Updated
Second Edition

Activity Book 5

with Online Resources

British English

Caroline Nixon & Michael Tomlinson

Cambridge University Press
www.cambridge.org/elt

Cambridge Assessment English
www.cambridgeenglish.org

Information on this title: www.cambridge.org/9781316628782

First published 2009
Second edition 2015
Updated second edition 2017

40 39 38 37 36 35 34 33 32 31 30 29 28 27 26 25 24 23 22 21 20

Printed in the Netherlands by Wilco BV

A catalogue record for this publication is available from the British Library

ISBN 978-1-316-62878-2 Activity Book with Online Resources 5
ISBN 978-1-316-62770-9 Pupil's Book 5
ISBN 978-1-316-62794-5 Teacher's Book 5
ISBN 978-1-316-62900-0 Class Audio CDs 5 (3 CDs)
ISBN 978-1-316-62947-5 Teacher's Resource Book with Online Audio 5
ISBN 978-1-316-62981-9 Interactive DVD with Teacher's Booklet 5 (PAL/NTSC)
ISBN 978-1-316-62804-1 Presentation Plus 5
ISBN 978-1-316-62856-0 Language Portfolio 5
ISBN 978-1-316-62871-3 Posters 5

Additional resources for this publication at www.cambridge.org/kidsbox

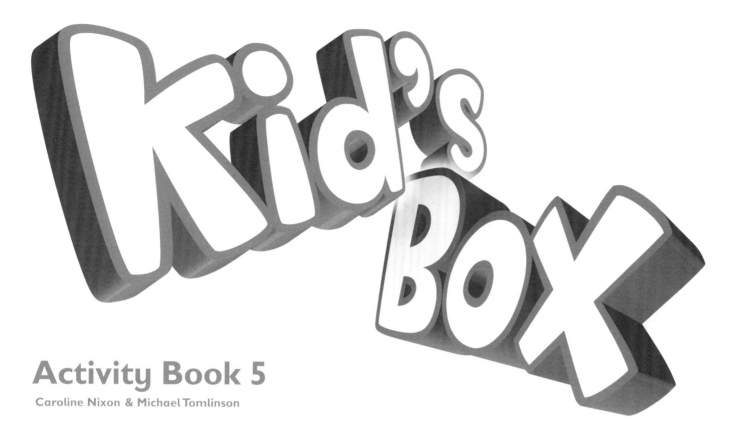

Kid's Box

Activity Book 5

Caroline Nixon & Michael Tomlinson

Welcome to our ezine

1 Put the words in groups.

book scarf program coat wifi comic screen
newspaper sweater trainers internet magazine

Things we read
book

Things we wear
scarf

Computer things
program

2 Match the sentences with Dan, Shari and Alvin.

1 I had a lovely holiday.

2 I'd like to write about sport.

3 We can write about anything in our ezine.

4 I'm new at school.

5 I live near Alvin.

6 I didn't know what an ezine was.

 ☐ ☐

  1 ☐

 ☐ ☐

3 Read and complete.

ezine videos music shops
magazine internet sports photos

An ezine is a kind of (1) magazine , but you
don't go to the (2) ------------------ to buy it. You can
do a search and find it on the (3) ------------------ .
You can read about football, tennis and other
(4) ------------------ . You can get information about
technology and the world around us. You can look at
lots of really interesting (5) ------------------ , listen
to all your favourite (6) ------------------ and watch
different kinds of (7) ------------------ . Shari, Dan and
Alvin write the new *Kid's Box* (8) ------------------ .
They want to win the school ezine competition.
There's a great prize!

4 Correct the sentences.

1 An ezine is a kind of book.
No, it isn't. It's a kind of _____
magazine. _____

2 You can find an ezine in the shops.
_____
_____

3 *Kid's Go* is a new ezine.
_____
_____

4 The three writers are called Sally,
Don and Alfred.
_____
_____

5 There's a prize for the worst ezine.
_____
_____

5 Read and order the text.

	ezine for young people. There are
	are Alvin, Shari and
9	Shari likes the natural world and drawing. She
	don't have to go to school.
	things. Alvin likes computers and sport, Dan
5	Dan. They all go to the same
	three writers. Their names
1	*Kid's Box* is an exciting new
	school: City School. They all like different
	really loves taking photos, too. They write
	likes music and clothes, and
	their ezine at the weekend when they

6 Read and complete the questions.

Where	When	~~What's~~
Why	How many	What

1 <u>What's</u>_____ the ezine called?
It's called *Kid's Box*.

2 _____ writers are there?
There are three.

3 _____'s the ezine about? **It's about the things that they like.**

4 _____ do they write the ezine? **They write it at the weekend.**

5 _____ do they write it then? **They write it then because they don't have to go to school.**

6 _____ can you see the ezine? **You can see it on the internet.**

7 Write the correct sentences.

~~Dan would like~~	oldest of	a village.
Dan	to school	~~music and clothes.~~
Shari walks	are both	Shari.
Alvin's the	lives near	the children.
Alvin	~~to write about~~	ten.
Dan and Shari	lives in	every day.

1 <u>Dan would like to write about music and clothes.</u>

2 _____

3 _____

4 _____

5 _____

6 _____

8 Choose words from the box to label the pictures.

| geography | language | history | maths | dictionary | ~~science~~ | music | exam |

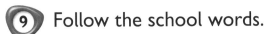

science _____ _____ _____ _____ _____ _____

9 Follow the school words.

classroom	sea	back	beans	cave	dress	rice
geography	history	potatoes	mountain	music	teacher	board
beard	maths	English	knee	sport	lake	subject
salad	river	computer studies	trousers	art	soup	ears
moustache	pasta	exam	dictionary	science	elbow	field

10 Now complete the table with words from Activity 9.

The body	**Food**	**The natural world**
elbow		

Two words are 'odd'? What are they? _____ _____

Which group are they from? _____

11 Answer the questions.

1 What's your school called? My school is called _____
2 What's your favourite subject? _____
3 What was your first subject yesterday? _____
4 Do you have lunch at school or at home? _____
5 What did you do after lunch yesterday? _____
6 Did you have any homework yesterday? _____

12 Read and complete the school timetable.

- Jim does these subjects at school: geography, history, music, maths, English, sport, computer studies, art, science.
- English is his last class on Mondays.
- His favourite day is Wednesday. He has sport at ten o'clock and music at eleven o'clock. He also has geography in the morning.
- Maths is his last class on Tuesdays and Wednesdays.
- On Thursdays his history class finishes at four o'clock and he has English at eleven o'clock.

- On Mondays he studies a lot. Before lunch he has maths after science and at eleven o'clock he has computer studies. After lunch he first has geography and then he has history.
- After science on Friday, Jim does these subjects in alphabetical order: history, sport, computer studies, music, English.
- The first class on Mondays and Fridays is the second class on Tuesdays.
- On Tuesdays the first class is computer studies. Before lunch he has geography and at two o'clock he has sport.
- He always has art after lunch, but not on Mondays or Fridays.
- He has music after art on Thursdays.
- He has science four times a week.

	Monday	Tuesday	Wednesday	Thursday	Friday
9.00–10.00				maths	science
10.00–11.00					
11.00–12.00					
lunch					
13.00–14.00					
14.00–15.00			English		
15.00–16.00					

13 Now write about Jim's timetable on Monday.

On Monday _____

_____

_____

_____

14 Write about your timetable on your favourite school day.

My favourite school day is _____

_____

_____

_____

15 Write the words in the columns.

January ~~children~~ watch village German French bridge dangerous question picture	'ch' (as in **ch**air)	'j' (as in **j**ump)
	children	

16 11 CD1 Listen, check and say.

17 Find 17 mistakes in the text.

❝❞ on mondays i have english, maths and history in the morning. after lunch i only have two lessons. they are science and art. art is my favourite subject. on tuesdays i don't have english or maths but i've got sport which is great. after sport i've got history and then in the afternoon i've got geography and science. i love doing experiments in science.

Punctuation – Capital letters and full stops
- Use capital (CAPITAL) letters at the start of sentences and for the names of people (David), the word 'I', places (London), days of the week (Monday) and languages (English).
- Use a full stop (.) at the end of a sentence.

Write it right

19 Write about your dream school timetable.

In my dream school timetable
I'd like to have

18 Now write the text correctly.

On Mondays

20 Read and answer.

1 Who's older: Sir Doug or Diggory Bones? <u>Sir Doug is older than Diggory.</u>
2 How long is the model dinosaur? _____
3 What are Diggory's students learning about? _____
4 What did The Rosetta Stone help us to do? _____
5 Where was Diggory's computer? _____
6 Who's Emily? _____

21 Read the text. Then look at the code and write the secret message.

Egyptian hieroglyphics were one of the first kinds of writing, but modern people couldn't understand them. Ancient people wrote important things on The Rosetta Stone in three different languages.

In 1822 a very clever man called Jean-François Champollion used two of the languages to understand the third, the Egyptian hieroglyphics. The Rosetta Stone helped us to understand the past better.

a	b	c	d	e	f	g	h	i	j	k	l	m

n	o	p	q	r	s	t	u	v	w	x	y	z

<u>V e r y</u> _____ _____ _____ _____ _____ _____ _____

_____. _____ _____ _____ _____ _____ _____ _____.

? Do you remember?

1 An internet magazine is called an <u>ezine</u> .
2 We use a _____ to find the meaning of words.
3 _____ is the school subject about different places in the world.
4 At school we learn about plants and the human body in _____ .
5 Two words with a 'ch' (as in '<u>ch</u>ildren') are _____ and _____ .
6 At the end of a sentence we use a _____ .

Can do
I can talk about school subjects.
I can ask my friends about their school timetable.
I can use capital letters and full stops.

LOOK again | The time

What's the time?
It's six o'clock.

(six) o'clock
five to (seven)
five past (six)
ten to (seven)
ten past (six)
quarter to (seven) → to | past ← **quarter past** (six)
twenty to (seven)
twenty past (six)
twenty-five to (seven)
twenty-five past (six)
half past (six)

1 Match the clocks with the pictures.

a | b | c | d | e | f [1]

1 | 2 Fun time | 3 | 4 | 5 The end | 6

2 Write the times.

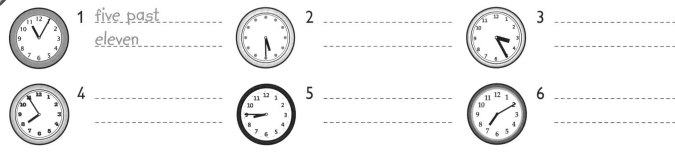

1 _five past_ _eleven_

2 _____

3 _____

4 _____

5 _____

6 _____

3 Read and draw the times on the clocks.

1 Bill wakes up at 7.10 on Mondays, Wednesdays and Fridays.
2 Nick leaves home at 8.55 in the morning.
3 Alex sometimes plays football at 15.30.
4 Anna always starts her homework at 16.00.
5 Tom watches his favourite programme on TV at 18.45 on Tuesdays and Thursdays.
6 Sue goes to bed at 21.00 every day.

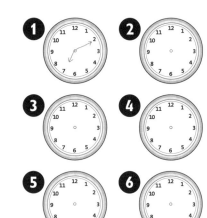

4 Match the clocks with the sentences for Dan's day yesterday. Put the sentences in order.

a He had lunch at half past twelve. _5_
b Classes started again at quarter to two. ___
c He caught a bus to school at twenty-five past eight. ___
d School finished at four o'clock. ___
e Dan caught the bus home at ten past four. ___

f Dan got dressed at ten to eight. ___
g He went out to the playground for break at quarter to eleven. ___
h Classes began at nine o'clock. ___

5 Find the past of these verbs and write them.

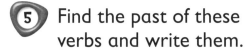

w	a	g	o	t	u	p	u
o	e	y	p	l	k	e	d
k	o	n	u	s	c	j	r
e	i	q	t	o	o	k	a
u	o	p	a	s	y	l	n
p	c	a	u	g	h	t	k
k	b	d	t	i	c	a	f
h	c	a	m	e	h	o	d

go   went
come   _____
have   _____
catch   _____
wake up   _____
get up   _____
eat   _____
drink   _____
put   _____
take   _____

6 Answer the questions about yesterday.

1 What time did you get up?
  I got up at _____
2 What time did you go to school?
  _____
3 Where did you have lunch?
  _____
4 What time did you go home?
  _____
5 What did you eat for dinner?
  _____
6 What did you drink in the evening?
  _____

7 Now choose your favourite day of last week and write about what you did.

_____ was my favourite day of last week.
_____
_____
_____

8 Choose words from the box to label the pictures.

| series | quiz | cartoon | comedy | ~~weather~~ | sport | news | documentary |

weather _____ _____ _____ _____ _____ _____

9 Write the programmes.

1 On this you can see swimming, basketball, tennis or motorbike racing. sport_____

2 This programme is funny, with funny people. _____

3 We watch this programme to see if today it is hot or cold. _____

4 This is on every day. It's about important things around the world. _____

5 A programme which tells us interesting facts about animals, history or places. _____

6 This programme has episodes and can be on TV every day. _____

10 Read and answer the questions.

Channel 1	Channel 2	Channel 3	Channel 4
12.10 Fun house (cartoon) 1.00 The news 1.45 The weather 2.15 Chelsea v Milan (football) 4.15 Animals of Africa (documentary)	11.50 Top songs (music videos) 12.30 Friendly (comedy) 2.10 Count to ten (quiz) 3.15 Giants v Bouncers (basketball)	12.30 The news 1.05 Explorers (documentary) 2.20 Annie get your gun (musical comedy film) 3.45 Cartoon hour	1.15 Maskman returns (film) 2.30 Our body (documentary) 3.15 Answer first (quiz) 3.55 Laugh out loud (comedy)

1 What time is the news on Channel 3? At 12.30._____

2 What channels are the cartoons on? _____

3 What's on Channel 1 at quarter to two? _____

4 What are the names of the two quiz programmes? _____

5 What are the documentaries about? (1) _____ , (2) _____ , (3) _____

6 What time is the film on Channel 4? _____

11 Write a TV page with your favourite programmes and times.

Channel 1	Channel 2	Channel 3	Channel 4
12.45 Sport today _____	_____ _____	_____ _____	_____ _____

12 Read and complete the table.

Now it's four o'clock. Four friends have got a problem because they can't decide which programme to watch.

- Sophia's favourite programme starts in 20 minutes and is called *Quacky Duck*. She likes cartoons, but doesn't like documentaries or sports programmes.
- The other girl, Emma, loves quiz programmes.
- *Who wants to be a billionaire?* started at 3.50.

- Frank loves playing sport and he likes watching it too. His favourite programme starts in 45 minutes.
- The other boy's favourite programme is called *World about us*. He's the only child who likes documentaries.
- The documentary starts at ten past four and the cartoon starts at twenty past four.
- Harry doesn't want to watch *Sunday sports*.
- Finally they all decide to watch Emma's favourite programme, but it started ten minutes ago!

Name	Sophia			
Kind of programme				
Programme name	Quacky Duck			
Programme time				

13 Now answer the questions.

1 Who doesn't like documentaries? Sophia, Emma and Frank
2 What's the name of the programme they decide to watch? ----
3 When did it start? ----
4 Whose favourite programme is it? ----
5 Who doesn't want to watch what's on TV at 4.45? ----
6 When does the cartoon start? ----

14 Answer the questions.

1 What's your favourite TV programme?
My favourite TV programme is ----
2 What kind of programme is it?
----
3 What time is it on?
----

15 How many words can you find in 'documentaries'?

star, mice, ----
----

16 Complete the sentences.

| Tuesday | university | ~~review~~ | usually | documentary | amazing |

1 After you see a film, you can write a <u>review</u> about it.
2 I _____ wake up at **8.30** in the morning.
3 Let's watch the _____ about monkeys on TV tonight.
4 On _____ afternoon the students have computer studies.
5 My sister is going to _____ next year.
6 Look at Daisy's _____ new jacket!

17 🔊 22 CD1 Listen, check and say.

18 Read the text and answer the questions.

Detective Will Hard is an amazing TV programme about a police officer and his adventures. He has to catch dangerous thieves in a big city. He's often in terrible situations. Ben Jones is the actor who plays the police officer. It's on Channel 4 at half past five on Saturday afternoons. I like this programme because it's really fast and exciting. There are lots of action scenes. The programme is funny, too. Detective Hard makes a lot of jokes.

Reviews
• A review is a text about something which you read or saw. You need to describe it and say what you thought about it.

• When you write a review you need to think about these questions: What? Where? When? Who?

• At the end of the review, you need to think about these questions: Do you like it? Why? / Why not?

Write it right

1 What's the TV programme called? <u>Detective Will Hard.</u>
2 What's it about? _____
3 Which actor's in it? _____
4 Which channel is it on? _____
5 What time is it on TV? _____
6 Why does he like it? _____

19 Use the questions and answers to write a review of a TV programme or film.

<u>I'm going to review a</u> _____
_____
_____
_____

20 Read and answer.

1 What's The Baloney Stone? _It's a computer program of old languages._

2 Where's The Baloney Stone? _____

3 What time did Emily turn on the TV? _____

4 Which programme did Diggory want to watch? _____

5 Who was the cameraman at the university? _____

6 What does Brutus Grabbe want? _____

21 Read the story so far and then write it in the past.

The story so far …

Diggory's in a classroom at the university. The reporter and the cameraman arrive. The reporter asks Diggory some questions. Diggory says that he doesn't want the thief to use The Baloney Stone to find treasure. At half past nine Diggory asks Emily to turn on the TV because he wants to watch the news. Brutus Grabbe comes onto the TV screen and laughs. He's the TV cameraman from the university! He wants Diggory's secret password for the computer program.

The story so far …
Diggory was in a classroom at the
university.
_____
_____
_____
_____
_____
_____
_____
_____
_____

? Do you remember?

1 The time in words is quarter to eleven. The time in numbers is _10.45_ .

2 The time in numbers is 8.25. The time in words is _____ .

3 A _____ is a TV programme which tells us interesting things about our world.

4 Two TV programmes that usually make us laugh are _____ and _____ .

5 Two words with a 'u' (as in 'u̱sually') are _____ and _____ .

6 At the _____ of the review you write about what you think.

Can do

I can tell the time in English.

I can talk about different kinds of TV programmes.

I can write a review of a TV programme.

History **Cartoons**

1 Answer the questions.

Cartoon questionnaire

1 What's your favourite comic? My favourite comic is _____
2 What's your favourite cartoon film? _____
3 Have you got any comic books? _____ . What are they called? _____
4 Have you got any cartoon films? _____ . What are they called? _____
5 Do you like cartoons? _____
6 Can you draw cartoons? _____
7 Do you prefer cartoons or films with actors? _____
8 Do you think that cartoons and comics are for grown-ups and children? _____

2 Answer 'yes' or 'no'.

1 The first cartoons were in colour. no_____
2 Mickey Mouse was in the first cartoon film with sound. _____
3 Donald Duck came before Mickey Mouse. _____
4 In the 1970s people used computers to make cartoons. _____
5 The first 3D film made using computers was *Toy Story*. _____
6 *Shrek* won a prize. _____

3 Plan a report about the history of animation.

Think about the answers to the questions above and about what you learned in the Pupil's Book.
You need: An introduction – What you are going to write about
          A middle   – What you learned
          An end   – The most interesting thing you found out

My plan

Introduction	Middle	End
I'm going to write about ...	I learned ...	The most interesting thing I found out is ...

4 Now write your report.

The history of animation
I'm going to write about the history of animation.

Listen and colour and write. There is one example.

2 People at work

LOOK again | **Going to**

We use *going to* to talk and write about the future.

Affirmative	Negative (n't = not)	Question
I'm **going to be** a nurse.	He **isn't going to be** a dentist.	**Is** he **going to be** an actor?
She**'s going to visit** me.	We **aren't going to do** it.	**Are** they **going to clean** it?

1 Write the words in the sentences.

| wear | ~~watch~~ | read | play | listen | be |

1 She's going to watch_____ TV after school.
2 He's going to _____ a fire fighter when he's older.
3 They aren't going to _____ a comic.
4 We're going to _____ to pop music.
5 I'm going to _____ my new trainers.
6 You aren't going to _____ badminton today.

2 Match the questions with the answers.

1	e	2		3		4		5		6		7		8	

1 How are you going to find the street?
2 What time's he going to get up?
3 Where are we going to have lunch?
4 Who are they going to talk to?
5 Which T-shirt are you going to wear?
6 Why's he going to go to the music festival?
7 When's she going to play basketball?
8 What are they going to do after school?

a They're going to talk to their friends.
b I'm going to wear my blue one.
c We're going to have it at home.
d He's going to listen to rock music.
e We're going to look at a map.
f He's going to get up at half past seven.
g They're going to do their homework.
h She's going to play on Saturday.

3 Look at this code. Write the secret message.

	1	2	3	4	5
1	a	b	c	d	e
2	f	g	h	i	j
3	k	l	m	n	o
4	p	q	r	s	t
5	u	v	w	x	y

a = 11, b = 21, c = 31

11-34-51   55-53-15   22-53-42-43-22   54-53   31-53-33-51
A r e   _ _ _   _ _ _ _ _ _   _ _   _ _ _ _ _

54-53   33-55   14-11-34-54-55?
_ _   _ _   _ _ _ _ _ _?

4 Now write another message for your friend in your notebook.

18

5 Look at the pictures and answer the questions.

1 **What are they going to do?** They're going to wash their clothes.
2 **What is she going to do?** _____
3 **What is he going to do?** _____
4 **What are they going to do?** _____
5 **What is he going to do?** _____
6 **What is she going to do?** _____

6 Make negative sentences.

1 He isn't going to catch the bus. _____ 4 _____
2 _____ 5 _____
3 _____ 6 _____

7 Look at Sam's diary for the weekend. Ask and answer the questions.

Friday	morning	School
	afternoon	4 pm Play football
Saturday	morning	10.45 Visit Grandma
	afternoon	2 pm Shopping for pyjamas
Sunday	morning	Walk in hills
	afternoon	4 pm Cinema

3 a) What time / Sam / visit his grandma
_____
b) _____

4 a) What / Sam / buy / Saturday afternoon
_____
b) _____

5 a) Where / Sam / walk / Sunday morning
_____
b) _____

6 a) What / Sam / do / Sunday afternoon
_____
b) _____

1 a) Where / Sam / go / Friday morning
Where's Sam going to go on Friday morning?
b) He's going to go to school.

2 a) What / Sam / do / Friday afternoon
_____
b) _____

8 Choose words from the box to label the pictures.

| mechanic | journalist | actor | ~~pilot~~ |
| football player | dancer | cook | manager |

1

pilot

2

_____

3

_____

4

_____

5

_____

6

_____

9 Complete the table.

person	verb
teacher	teach
	drive
dancer	
	skate
	design
	sing
	paint
	photograph
manager	
tennis player	
runner	
	swim

10 Read and write the words in the puzzle.

1 Someone who drives buses.
   A bus driver _____ .
2 Someone who works with food.
   A _____ .
3 Someone who stops fires.
   A _____ .
4 Someone who looks after our teeth.
   A _____ .
5 Someone who works in a hospital.
   A _____ .
6 Someone who flies planes.
   A _____ .
7 Someone who repairs cars.
   A _____ .
8 Someone who paints pictures.
   An _____ .
9 Someone who acts in films.
   An _____ .

1 | b | u | s | d | r | i | v | e | r |
2 _____ | s |
3 _____ | | | |
4 _____ |
5 _____ |
6 _____ |
7 _____ |
8 _____ |
9 _____ |

What's the mystery job? _____

11 Now write a definition for this job.

_____
_____
_____

20

12 These four children are going to have different jobs. Write the numbers.

a □ □ □   b □ □ □   c 1 □ □   d □ □ □

1 He's going to fly planes.
2 He's going to travel a lot.
3 He's going to repair cars.
4 She's going to use eggs.
5 He's going to get dirty.
6 She's going to wear a white hat.

7 He's going to visit lots of airports.
8 She's going to work in a kitchen.
9 She's going to look after people's teeth.
10 He's going to work with machines.
11 She's going to tell children not to eat sweets.
12 She's going to wear gloves and a mask.

13 Slim Jim's a famous singer. Read and complete his diary.

1 He's going to meet his manager after lunch on Friday.
2 The same day that he sings, he's going to open a new school in the morning.
3 He's going to go to the cinema next Thursday afternoon.
4 After lunch on the day he arrives in London, he's going to talk to some children who are in hospital.
5 He's going to have a TV interview before lunch on the day he goes to the cinema.

6 He arrives at London airport next Monday morning.
7 On the same day that he's having dinner with some actors, he's going to visit a music shop in the morning.
8 He's going to sing in a big football stadium.
9 He's flying to Spain in the morning of the same day that he's going to meet his manager.
10 He's going to have dinner with some actors next Tuesday evening.

	Monday	Tuesday	Wednesday	Thursday	Friday
a.m.	-----	-----	-----	-----	-----
	lunch	lunch	lunch	lunch	lunch
p.m.	-----	-----	-----	-----	meet manager

14 Answer the questions.

1 Where are you going to go after school this afternoon? I'm going to go _____
2 Who are you going to see this evening? _____
3 When are you going to do your homework? _____
4 What time are you going to go to bed tonight? _____

15 Can you remember? Complete the sentences.

doctor ~~older~~ answer
picture stronger treasure

1 The manager is <u>older</u> than the actor.
2 The swimmer is _____ than the writer.
3 The farmer found some _____ .
4 The teacher showed her students a _____ .
5 The _____ is writing on some paper.
6 The dancer knows the _____ .

16 Listen, check and say.

17 Find 14 mistakes in the text.

My dad's job
My dads a cook in a restaurant. Its called Petes Diner. The restaurants big. Its got more than 20 tables and five cooks. Dad likes his job, but he doesnt have many holidays. He isnt working today, but hes cooking dinner for me and my sister. He doesnt always cook at home because hes often tired when he finishes work. Mums a great cook too, but she doesnt get any money for cooking. Shes a history teacher.

18 Now write the text correctly.

My dad's job

Punctuation – The apostrophe
We use an apostrophe:
• to show a letter or letters are missing when we join two words (*do not = don't, I have = I've*).

• to show possession (*John's book*).

Write it right

19 Write about a job someone in your family does.

My _____ 's a _____
_____
_____
_____
_____
_____
_____
_____
_____
_____
_____
_____
_____
_____

20 Read and answer.

1 What's Diggory's job? _He's an archaeologist._
2 Where does Brutus want Diggory to meet him?

_____

3 Why did Diggory call him 'a pirate'? _____
4 What time are Diggory and Emily going to meet Brutus? _____
5 Is Brutus at the library? _____
6 Who's got a letter for Diggory? _____

21 Read and order the text.

ancient languages. Brutus Grabbe took it from ☐

The Baloney Stone is a very important computer | 1 |

at the Old City Library at 10.45, but Brutus wasn't there. ☐

program which can help us to understand ☐

has got the program, but he wants Diggory's ☐

secret password. Brutus went on the evening news ☐

on TV to speak to Diggory. He told him to meet him ☐

Diggory's classroom at the university. Now Brutus ☐

? Do you remember?

1 A _pilot_ flies planes.
2 A mechanic _____ cars.
3 When people have problems with their teeth, they see a _____ .
4 We use '_____ _____' to talk and write about the future.
5 Two words with a short 'er' (as in 'doct<u>or</u>') are _____
   and _____ .
6 We use an apostrophe to show a _____ is missing when we join two words.

Can do   I can use *going to* to talk about the future.
             I can talk about people at work.
             I can use apostrophes.

☹ ☺ ☺
☹ ☺ ☺
☹ ☺ ☺

23

1 Teeth quiz. Read and choose the right words.

1 The teeth we have when we are young are called
  a) juice teeth.   b) (milk teeth.)   c) wisdom teeth.

2 How many different types of teeth have we got?
  a) three   b) four   c) five

3 The hard part on the outside of our teeth is called
  a) crown.   b) root.   c) enamel.

4 We use our incisors to
  a) cut our food.   b) chew our food.   c) drink.

5 Molars are at the
  a) side of our mouth. b) front of our mouth. c) back of our mouth.

6 The part of the teeth in our gums is called
  a) the enamel.   b) the crown.   c) the root.

2 Complete the teeth mind map.

> brush for two minutes   milk teeth   drink milk   go twice every year
> eat carrots and apples   brush twice a day   permanent teeth   listen
> don't drink sugary drinks   rinse with water

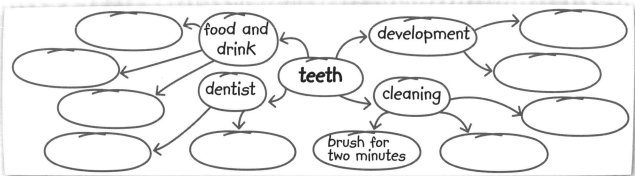

3 Answer the questions.

1 How many teeth have you got? I've got

2 Have you got any milk teeth?

3 How old were you when you got your first permanent tooth?

4 Do you like going to the dentist?

5 What does the dentist say to you?

6 What do you do to look after your teeth?

4 Use the answers to write about your teeth.

My teeth
I've got   teeth.

5 Read the letter and write the missing words. Write one word on each line.

Example

Dear KBTV,

Last Saturday I saw something on your channel
about a new quiz show for young people. It's
called........................... 'Boxing Clever'.
I wrote to you last year about a different
programme, but you needed people who were

1   older .... me. I think this new
quiz show is for children of my age, and we have

2   to .... questions about different

3   school subjects. I'm very .... at
geography and history, but science is my best
subject.

4   I would like .... go on the quiz
show. Please can you send me

5   .... more information so that I
can show my parents?

From
Robert Brown

Review Units  1 and 2

1 Read the story. Choose words from the box to complete the sentences.

> channel painted history quiz fire fighter time going documentary
> jobs ~~programme~~

Friendly

Friendly is a really funny comedy (1) <u>programme</u> . It's on TV at twenty to five every day. In this show there are five friends who all go to the same school in a big city. They live and study in the school, but they aren't all in the same class.

They're all going to have different (2) _____ when they grow up. Peter wants to be a cook, Jenny wants to be an actor, Sally wants to be a taxi driver, Jim wants to be a (3) _____ and Sue wants to be an artist.

In the story last week, Sue (4) _____ a picture for an art competition and Jenny sat as a model for her. In the picture which Sue painted, Jenny had one square eye, which was red, and a carrot for a nose. One of her legs was a mobile phone and the other was a banana. Sue's friends don't think she's (5) _____ to win the competition, but Sue's happy. She knows she isn't going to be a famous artist!

2 Choose a title for this episode of *Friendly*.

a) Modern art
b) Fun and games
c) Beautiful people

3 Draw and colour Sue's painting.

4 Match the questions with the answers.

1	Why do zebras like old films?		An eggzam!
2	What goes up slowly and comes down quickly?		When there are two of them!
3	What's a chicken's most important test at school?		B.
4	What do you call bears with no ears?	1	Because they're in black and white.
5	What's always slow to come, but never arrives?		An elephant in a lift!
6	When do elephants have eight feet?		Tomorrow.

5 Complete the sentences. Count and write the letters.

1 An internet magazine is called an _ezine_____ . | 5 |
2 The study of the past is called _____ .
3 Eight fifteen is _____ past eight.
4 The lesson when we draw and paint is _____ .
5 Good, better, _____ .
6 The study of different countries is called _____ .
7 A competition with questions is a _____ .
8 Somebody who repairs cars is a _____ .
9 Something we study at school is called a _____ .
10 A manager works on this in an office. A _____ .
11 Eleven thirty is _____ past eleven.
12 The study of numbers is called _____ .
13 Somebody who paints pictures is an _____ .
14 The opposite of work is _____ .

6 Now complete the crossword. Write the message.

|3|

|2| e | z | i | n | e |

|4|

|6|

|1|

|5|

| 1 | 2 | 3 | 3 | 4 | | 5 | 1 | 2 | 6 | 2 |
| | e | | | | | | | e | | e |

7 Quiz time!

1 What languages can they study at City School? _They can study_____
_____

2 In this lesson we learn about plants and the human body.
_____

3 In a cartoon, how many pictures do they use for one second of film?
_____

4 What does Shari think she's going to be?
_____

5 What jobs did George Orwell have?
_____

6 How many kinds of teeth have we got?
_____

8 Write questions for your quiz in your notebook.

3 City life

right ➡   left ⬅   straight on ⬆   corner ↰

past ⬆   across ⬆   along ⬅

1 Read and answer the questions.

Yesterday afternoon five people got on a bus at the bus station: one man, two women and two children. The bus left the station at nine o'clock. It had to stop at the corner because the traffic lights were red. The bus turned left after the traffic lights.

The bus didn't stop at the first bus stop, but drove straight on because there weren't any people waiting there and no one wanted to get off. The bus turned right at the next corner and drove over the bridge. At the second bus stop, outside the school, the two children and the man got off and nine more people got on. Then the bus went into the train station, where ten people got off and 12 more got on. The bus drove out of the station, turned left and went straight on to the end of the road.

1 How many people got off at the second stop? _____

2 How many times did the bus turn left? _____

3 How many people were there on the bus when it drove out of the train station? _____

2 Tick (✓) or cross (✗) the sentences.

1 Yesterday morning six people got on at the bus station: two men, one woman and three children. _____

2 The bus had to stop at the corner because the traffic lights were red. _____

3 After the first bus stop, it turned left at the next corner. _____

4 At the second bus stop, outside the hospital, the two children and the man got off. _____

3 Read and complete the sentences.

along	left	on the corner
straight on	right	~~across~~

1 She ran *across* the park.

2 She turned _____ at the corner of Queen Street.

3 He went _____ at the traffic lights.

4 He waited for his friend _____ outside the school.

5 He turned _____ into King Street.

6 He walked _____ Prince Street.

4 Follow the directions and write the message.

London	to	29	places	million	is
of	see	the	interesting	in	and
lots	are	year	visit	people	every
biggest	There	UK.	it.	city	the

r = right   l = left   u = up   d = down

London – 5r – 3d – 5l – 4r – 2u – 2l – 2d –1l – 1u – 1l – 1u – 3r – 1u – 2l – 1d – 4r – 1d – 3l – 2u – 2r – 2d – 1l – 1d

London _____ _____ _____ _____ _____ _____

_____ _____ _____ _____ _____ _____

_____ _____ _____ _____ _____ _____

_____ _____ _____ _____ _____ _____

5 Put these buildings on the map.

1 The gym's on the right of the supermarket.
2 The cinema's opposite the bus station.
3 The castle's opposite the car park.
4 The library's between the café and the toyshop.
5 The school's on the other side of the road from the bookshop and opposite the hospital.
6 The bookshop's behind the fire station.
7 The stadium's on the other side of the road from the bookshop, on the corner.

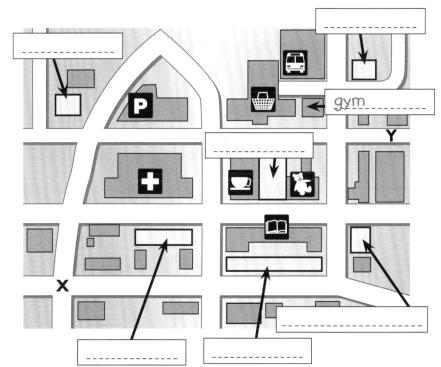

6 Find these buildings in Activity 5.

1 Start at the X. Go straight on and take the first road on the right. Go past the hospital and the café. It's the building on the left before the toy shop. What is it? _____

2 Start at the X. Turn right and walk to the fire station. Go past the fire station and walk to the next corner. Turn left. It's on the corner on the right. What is it? _____

7 Now write two sets of directions for a friend to follow.

1 Start at the X. Go ...

8 Choose words from the box to label the pictures.

| museum | post office | ~~hotel~~ | airport | restaurant | castle | theatre | police station |

1 **2** **3** **4** **5** **6**

<u>hotel</u>_____ _____ _____ _____ _____ _____

9 Sort and write the words.

1 prrtaio <u>airport</u>_____ 2 eatther _____ 3 letsac _____

4 aeiiolonpsttc _____ 5 sumemu _____ 6 ethol _____

10 Complete the table. Look in the Pupil's Book to find the names of the places.

Yesterday Paul visited London with his family. They went to seven different places.
• At nine o'clock Paul went to a place where you can see exciting things from all over the world.
• They went for a boat trip on the River Thames at half past ten.
• After lunch they went to the place where Shakespeare and his actors showed their plays.
• They took a taxi from Tower Bridge at half past five and went back to their hotel.
• They had a picnic lunch at quarter to one. They ate some sandwiches in Hyde Park.
• After visiting the theatre, they went to look at an old building next to Tower Bridge.
• They arrived at the oldest hotel in London at ten to six. They had dinner and went to bed.

9.00	Went to the British Museum.
10.30	
2.30	
4.30	
5.50	

11 Look at the letters on the clock and write the words.

1 It's five to one. <u>straight</u>_____

2 It's eight o'clock. _____

3 It's ten to six. _____

4 It's ten past nine. _____

5 It's twenty-five past four. _____

6 It's twenty-five to three. _____

sch
stra   ight
st   p
ark   •   oad
ool   op
r   sh
adium

12 Write 'who', 'which' or 'where'.

1 A place _where___ you can buy stamps.
2 Someone _____ flies planes.
3 Something _____ you have to buy when you go by bus or train.
4 A place _____ we go to see a play.
5 Someone _____ cooks food in a restaurant.
6 A place _____ you can see old paintings and books.
7 A place _____ you can catch a plane.
8 A place _____ you can get money.
9 Someone _____ repairs cars.
10 A place _____ you go to cross a river.

13 Now find the words from Activity 12.

a	c	e	t	u	r	e	d	p	m
i	q	p	i	l	o	t	b	m	u
r	c	y	c	s	z	a	r	e	s
p	o	s	t	o	f	f	i	c	e
o	b	p	h	d	o	v	d	h	u
r	o	a	e	u	l	k	g	a	m
t	m	k	n	o	a	n	e	n	y
c	a	w	t	k	r	o	t	i	p
f	t	b	r	t	p	i	e	c	o
s	u	c	e	t	i	c	k	e	t

14 Write a definition of these words.

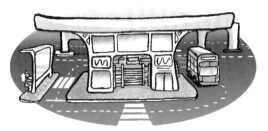

1 A place _____
_____ .

2 Someone _____
_____ .

15 Put these places on your map.

castle	bank	hotel	airport
restaurant		museum	theatre

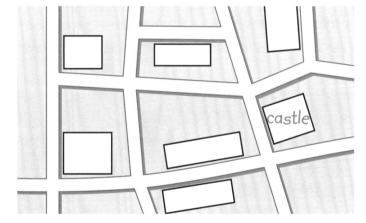

castle

16 Now write directions from the castle to three places on the map.

1 Start at the castle. Go ...

17 Ask your friend to follow your directions.

18 Write the words in the columns.

shopping	listen	children	information	stop	castle	watched	machine
place	question	adventure	directions				

's' (as in **s**un)	'sh' (as in **sh**e)	'ch' (as in **ch**ips)
listen		

19 Listen, check and say.

20 Find 15 spelling mistakes in the text.

In this picture we can see lots of children playeing. Three boyes are siting on the ground and plying with their toyes. They've got some toy lorrys and a buss. They're near two ladys who are sitinng on chairs. These ladys are the boiys' mums. Some older children are flyng their kites. One boye's kite is in a tree. He's climmbing up the tree and he's trieing to get it down.

Write it right

22 Describe your school playground.

In our school playground we can see

21 Now write the text correctly.

In this picture we can see lots of children playing.

23 Read and answer.

1 Why was it the wrong library? _Because it was the wrong city._
2 Which city does Brutus mean? _____
3 What are they going to do now? _____
4 What is there outside Alexandria? _____
5 What's on the walls of the cave? _____
6 Who's the taxi driver? _____

24 Who said it? Read and match.

1    **2**    **3**    **4**

a I think he means the city of Alexandria in Egypt. `1`

b Brutus can use The Baloney Stone to understand the writing! ☐

c What are we going to do now? ☐

d … can open the door to mountains of secret treasure! ☐

e Now let's get a taxi and find a hotel. ☐

f Yes, son. ☐

? **Do you remember?**

1 An actor sometimes works in a _theatre_____ .
2 You can stay in a _____ when you go on holiday.
3 Be careful when you walk _____ the road. Look out for cars!
4 The opposite of 'turn right' is 'turn _____' .
5 Two words with a 'sh' (as in '<u>she</u>') are _____ and _____ .
6 One leaf, two _____ .

Can do   I can talk about places around town.
I can give and understand directions.
I can spell plural nouns.

😞 😐 🙂
😞 😐 🙂
😞 😐 🙂

33

1 City quiz. Read and choose the right words.

1 The capital city of the USA is   a) New York.   b) Los Angeles.   c) Washington DC.
2 Paris is the capital city of   a) Japan.   b) Australia.   c) France.
3 The only city in two continents is   a) Istanbul.   b) Moscow.   c) Cairo.
4 In 1900 the biggest city in the world was   a) Rome.   b) New York.   c) London.
5 The first cities in the world were in
   a) the Amazon Valley.   b) the Indus Valley.   c) the Thames Valley.
6 People started living in cities
   a) to buy and sell food.   b) to catch the bus.   c) because they didn't like farming.

2 Read this report about Stratford-upon-Avon.

Stratford-upon-Avon is a town near Birmingham in England. About 25,000 people live here. The city is more than 800 years old. It's famous because William Shakespeare was born here. He wrote lots of plays, including *Romeo and Juliet* and *Macbeth*. You can still see his plays today in the Royal Shakespeare Theatre. There are lots of other interesting different places to go. Children can go to the museum, the library, the sports centre, the cinema and the park. The town has also got a bus and train station. I like Stratford-upon-Avon because the river is beautiful. The only thing I don't like is that it takes a long time to travel to the beach.

3 Complete the Stratford-upon-Avon mind map.

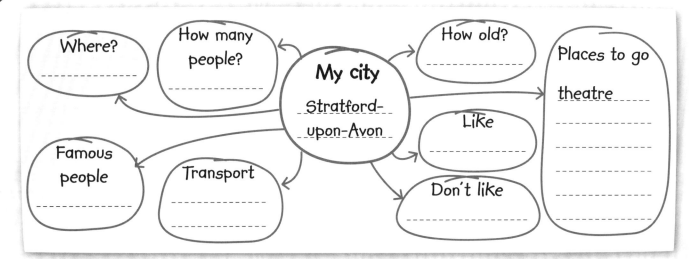

4 Now draw a mind map about your town or city.

5 Use the information from Activity 4 to write your report.

My city

Listen and write. There is one example.

George's holiday to London

	Transport:	by ..train..............................
1	Hotel name:	The ....
2	Where the hotel is:	next to the British ....
3	Hotel phone number:	....
4	Where George visited:	The .... Theatre
5	Time of the play:	Sunday at ....

4 Disaster!

We use the past continuous to describe what was happening in the past.

Affirmative	Negative (n't = not)	Question
I **was listening** to music.	You **weren't playing** tennis.	**Was** she **reading**?
They **were walking** to school.	He **wasn't running** in the park.	**Were** they **sailing**?

1 Match the pictures with the text.

Emma's talking to her teacher. She's saying why she was late for school.

☐ Then I saw the bus. It was coming down the street so I started to run.

☐ The books were on the road in the water when the bus ran over them.

☐ I didn't have a coat or umbrella so I decided to get the bus.

☐ Now I can't find my homework. It must be on the road. Sorry! And I'm sorry I'm late!

[1] I had a disaster this morning. I was walking to school when it started to rain.

☐ When I was running for the bus I dropped my schoolbag and my books fell out on to the road.

2 Write the verbs in the table. Look at the spelling.

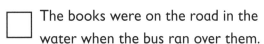

~~move~~   cut   stop   live   enjoy   wake up
shout   lose   cook   swim   carry   get

tak**ing** (🖊 + -ing)	sail**ing** (+ -ing)	ru**nn**ing (x2 + -ing)
moving		

3 Read and choose the right words.

1 They were sailing across the lake **when** / **because** it started to rain.
2 He was **climb** / **climbing** in the mountains when it started to snow.
3 My dad was having a shower when the phone **ring** / **rang**.
4 The boy **was** / **were** flying his kite when he hurt his elbow.
5 They were losing **if** / **when** he scored the goal.

4 Write questions and answers about Paul's day.

1 What was Paul doing at twenty past three?   He was catching the bus.

2 _____   _____

3 _____   _____

4 _____   _____

5 _____   _____

6 _____   _____

5 Read and complete the table.

Last week somebody broke a chair in the classroom during playtime. The children don't want to tell the teacher who broke the chair, so the teacher is trying to find out.

David was wearing a red sweater and a long scarf. Betty was wearing a short skirt and green shoes. Katy was wearing jeans and a T-shirt. William was wearing grey trousers and a blue shirt.

One girl was jumping around the classroom. One of the boys was playing football outside. One girl was reading a book in the playground. David was talking to his friends in the playground. The child who broke the chair wasn't wearing green shoes or grey trousers.

Name	David			
Clothes				
Where?				
What doing?				

Who broke the chair? _____ .

6 Choose dates from the box to label the pictures.

26 August 1883   ~~1 November 1755~~   6 May 1937   14 April 1912
28 December 1908   10 October 1780

1 November 1755   _____   _____   _____   _____   _____

7 Read and write the dates.

1 The day before the twenty-fifth.
The twenty-fourth.

2 The day after the twenty-first.
_____

3 The day after the twenty-fourth.
_____

4 This day is three days after the twenty-sixth.
_____

5 This is the day after the twenty-third.
_____

6 This day is three days before the thirtieth.
_____

8 Complete the sentences.

1 The first month is January .
2 The third month is _____ .
3 The fifth month is _____ .
4 The seventh month is
_____ .
5 The eleventh month is
_____ .
6 The twelfth month is _____ .

9 Sort and write the months. Put them in order.

~~gjaaunr~~   frbryeua   charm   lipar
yam   juen   uyjl   atuugs   restebpem
boorcte   mnborvee   redbeemc

			1	2	3	4
5	6	7	8	9	10	11
12	13	14	15	16	17	18
19	20	21	22	23	24	25
26	27	28	29	30	31	

☐ A _ _ _ _

☐ S _ _ _ _ _ _ _ _

☐ M _ _ _ _ _

☐ M _ _

1 J a n u a r y

☐ A _ _ _ _ _

☐ J _ _ e

☐ O _ _ _ _ _ _ _

☐ D _ _ _ _ _ _ _

☐ J _ _ _ _

☐ N _ _ _ _ _ _ _ _

☐ F _ _ _ _ _ _ _ _

10 Answer the questions.

1 What date was it yesterday? It was _____
2 What date is it going to be next Saturday? _____
3 When's your birthday? _____
4 When's your friend's birthday? _____
5 When's your teacher's birthday? _____
6 What date does school finish this term? _____

11 Match the words with the pictures.

1 storm   **2** tsunami   **3** ice   **4** hurricane

[ ]	1	[ ]	[ ]
[ ]	[ ]	[ ]	[ ]

5 volcano   **6** fog   **7** fire   **8** lightning

12 Now match the words and pictures with the definitions.

a Heavy rain and strong winds. [1]

b Very cold water which is solid, not liquid. [ ]

c A mountain with a big hole at the top through which liquid rock and hot gas can come out. [ ]

d Electricity in the air which passes from one cloud to another or to the ground. [ ]

e Burning material and gases which can burn other things. [ ]

f A cloud which is near the ground or the sea. [ ]

g An enormous and fast wave. [ ]

h This is the worst kind of storm, with very strong winds and heavy rain. [ ]

13 Keep a weather diary.

Date	sun	wind	cloud	storm	rain	snow	fog
Monday _____							

14 Write the words in the columns.

| story | storm | disaster | terrible | stopped | wanted | decided | dangerous |

1 ●	**2** ●●	**3** ●●●	**4** ●●●
storm			

 15 **22 CD2** Listen, check and say.

16 Find the 22 past simple and past continuous verbs
and 4 sequencing words in this story.

My favourite film of the year (was) *Detective Will Hard 2*. This is what (happened) in the most exciting scene of the film.

The thieves (were running) after Detective Hard. He (had) to jump off a really high building to escape. (Then) he jumped onto a lorry, which was full of black plastic bags, but the baddies got onto a motorbike and started to follow him. The motorbike was much faster so it wasn't long before it was next to the lorry on the road. One of the thieves was trying to climb up the side of the lorry when Hard jumped off it and onto the back of the motorbike. The driver and Hard were fighting as they went over a bridge. Then Hard pushed the driver off the motorbike into the river. After that he quickly stopped the bike before it hit a bus. Next he called another police officer on his mobile and pulled the thief out of the river. He said, 'Water you doing here?' Everybody laughed.

Reviews
- When we write a story, we think about what happened, where and when it happened and who was there. For this we use verbs in the past simple.
- Then we describe what was happening at the same time. This makes the story more interesting. For this we use verbs in the past continuous.
- We use connecting words like *and*, *but* and *because*. We also use sequencing words like *then*, *next* and *after that*.

Write it right

17 Answer the questions.

1 What was the film called? <u>Detective Will Hard 2.</u>
2 Where was Detective Hard at the beginning of the scene? _____
3 What was happening as they went over the bridge? _____
4 Who fell in the river? _____
5 What happened at the end of the scene? _____
_____

 18 Write about a scene from your favourite film.

My favourite film is called ...

40

19 Read and answer.

1 What does 'Canis Major' mean? _It means 'the big dog'._
2 What's the brightest star called? _____
3 What was the date in the story? _____
4 When did Diggory remember the disaster? _____
5 What destroyed Ancient Alexandria? _____
6 What came after the volcanic eruption? _____

20 Complete the sentences from the story. Match them with the pictures.

light	~~date~~	dangerous
hot	storm	secret

1 What's the _date_ today, Emily?
2 Night's falling and a _____'s coming.
3 Is it too _____ for you, Bones?
4 Today, it's going to show us the 'opening' of the _____ cave!
5 It's really _____ down here.
6 Run to the _____, Emily!

? **Do you remember?**

1 It's very difficult to see when the weather is _foggy_ .
2 We sometimes see _____ in the sky when there's a storm.
3 Today's date in numbers is _____ .
4 Tomorrow's date in words is _____ .
5 Two words which have stress on the first syllable are _____ and _____ .
6 We use connecting words like _____ and _____ when we tell stories.

Can do
I can talk about the weather and disasters.
I can talk about things that were happening in the past.
I can tell a story.

Geography   The Earth's surface

1 Disasters quiz. Read and choose the right words.

1 Natural disasters happen because of
   a) people.   b) land moving.
   c) natural forces.
2 Earthquakes and tsunamis happen near
   a) plate boundaries.   b) rock.
   c) crust.
3 Earthquakes happen when plates move
   a) slowly.   b) all day.   c) suddenly.

4 The Richter Scale is used to measure
   a) hurricanes.   b) earthquakes.
   c) tsunamis.
5 A tsunami is lots of enormous
   a) fish.   b) earthquakes.   c) waves.
6 Most tsunamis occur in the
   a) Atlantic Ocean.
   b) Pacific Ocean.   c) Indian Ocean.

2 Choose words from the box to complete the text.

| boat | earthquake | underwater | Ocean | dangerous |
| hours | ~~Japanese~~ | hundred | rock | minutes |

The word 'tsunami' comes from the (1) Japanese word meaning 'harbour wave'. A tsunami happens when a lot of water is moved under the sea by an (2) _____ , volcano or other disaster. Most tsunamis are because of (3) _____ earthquakes, but not all earthquakes cause tsunamis – an earthquake has to be over 6.75 to cause a tsunami. Nine out of ten tsunamis happen in the Pacific (4) _____ . A tsunami can travel at seven (5) _____ kilometres an hour. When a tsunami hits land, it can be very (6) _____ .

3 Find out about a volcano, tsunami or earthquake. Make notes about it.

What?
Where?
Facts:
Disaster:

4 Now use the information to write your report.

My report

5 Emma's talking to her friend David about what he did last night.
What does David say to Emma?

Read the conversation and choose the best answer.
Write a letter (A–E) for each answer.

There is one example.

Example

 Emma: Did you watch TV last night?

David: D ....

Questions

1 **Emma:** What did you watch?

David: ....

2 **Emma:** What was it about?

David: ....

3 **Emma:** Really, was there anything on earthquakes?

David: ....

4 **Emma:** What time did it finish?

David: ....

A Yes, there was. It was really amazing.

B I watched a documentary.

C It wasn't late. It finished at 7 o'clock.

D Yes, I did. **(Example)**

E It was all about natural disasters.

Review Units 3 and 4

1 Read the story. Choose words from the box to complete the sentences.

left	~~March~~	straight	walking	restaurant	quarter	wasn't	corner
theatre	were	right					

Friendly

Last Saturday, 30 (1) _March_____ , was Jim's birthday. He decided to go to the city centre with Peter to have lunch in an expensive (2) _____ and to go to the cinema to see a film. They went to the station at (3) _____ past nine on Saturday morning and caught the train from platform 1. They didn't know the city very well and they didn't have a map so they decided to explore. When they were walking along a long road, they turned (4) _____ , not right, and got lost. When they were trying to find the right street, they saw hotels, post offices, gyms and museums, but no restaurants. At ten past two, they found a small café. They were really hungry, so they stopped there and had a burger and chips for lunch. When they got to the cinema, they found it (5) _____ showing the action film they wanted to see – it was showing a cartoon about funny animals for very young children.

They were (6) _____ back to the station when it started to rain heavily and they didn't have any coats. Jim thought that his birthday was the biggest disaster ever, but then Peter started to laugh loudly and they agreed it was the funniest birthday ever.

2 Choose a title for this episode of *Friendly*.

a) The best day   b) The wrong map   c) What a disaster!

3 Find the odd one out.

1 across   past   (museum)   behind
   _Museum because it's a building._____
   _____

2 hotel   taxi   restaurant   theatre
   _____
   _____

3 stadium   left   between   right
   _____
   _____

4 lightning   rain   snow   tsunami
   _____
   _____

5 sailed   ran   flew   help
   _____
   _____

6 February   Thursday   April   October
   _____
   _____

4 Complete the sentences. Count and write the letters.

1 This is smaller than a road. It's a <u>street</u>_____ .   **6**

2 The lightning _____ their boat.   ☐

3 The opposite of inside is _____ .   ☐

4 The tenth month is _____ .   ☐

5 There was a forest _____ last summer. It burned everything.   ☐

6 The place where we go to catch a plane is an _____ .   ☐

7 Cloud on the ground is called _____ .   ☐

8 The month that comes before September is _____ .   ☐

9 There's a _____ when there's heavy rain and a strong wind.   ☐

10 We go to a _____ to see old books and paintings.   ☐

11 We use a _____ to help us find our way.   ☐

12 The point where two streets meet is a _____ .   ☐

13 We need a _____ to walk over a river.   ☐

14 The first month is _____ .   ☐

5 Now complete the crossword. Write the message.

1	2	3	4	4	2	1		5	6	4	5	7	
s						s							**!**

6 Quiz time!

1 What's the name of the busiest airport in the world? <u>The busiest airport is</u>____
_____

2 When was Mohenjo-Daro built?
_____

3 What was Dan listening to on the boat?
_____

4 What happened on 6 May 1937?
_____

5 What does the Richter Scale measure?
_____

7 Write questions for your quiz in your notebook.

45

5 Material things

LOOK again | Made of

We use *made of* to describe materials.

Affirmative	Negative (n't = not)	Question
It's **made of** chocolate.	It isn't **made of** paper.	Is it **made of** sugar?
They're **made of** stone.	They aren't **made of** wood.	Are they **made of** leaves?

1 Match the words with the pictures.

> grass   leaves   paper   ~~bone~~
> stone   brick

1

bone

2

3

_____   _____

4

5

6

_____   _____   _____

2 Read and order the words.

1 made / This / is / jacket / fur. / of
   This jacket is made of fur.

2 isn't / skirt / That / made / chocolate. / of
   _____

3 your / of? / sweater / made / What's
   _____

4 T-shirt / your / Is / of / made / fur?
   _____

5 made / of / their / shoes / Are / wood?
   _____

6 paper. / clothes / made / are / of / His
   _____

3 Answer the questions.
   What are they made of?

 1 They're made of chocolate.

 2 _____

 3 _____

 4 _____

 5 _____

 6 _____

4 Correct the sentences.

1 My hats is made of fur.

2 The spider has made of paper.

3 The cake aren't made of chocolate.

4 Is his jacket made off rubber?

5 Are their houses mades of stone?

6 My sweets is made of sugar.

5 Write the correct sentences.

Our house	made	of paper.
The boat is	is made	of rubber.
My book's	are made	of stone.
Their tyres	made of	wood.

1 _____
2 _____
3 _____
4 _____

6 Read, look and label the picture.

My house is made of trees and it's got grass on the roof. Grass is really good because it's very green. The house stays hot in the winter and cold in the summer. When it snows, I can ski on it!
The door is made of wood. The windows are made of water bottles. When it rains, the water from the roof goes into the window bottles. I use it to water my plants. There are leaves over the balcony. I can sit under these when it's sunny.

1 house made of trees _____

2 _____
_____

3 _____

4 _____

5 _____
_____

7 Read and complete the text.

| bottles | bridges | thousand | ~~materials~~ | stone | gold |

The Romans were the first people to use a lot of different
(1) materials _____ , both for building and in their everyday life. They were very good at making things from a lot of different metals, including
(2) _____ and silver.

They made a lot of things with glass, like (3) _____ and glasses for drinking.

The Romans made houses from wood, (4) _____ and concrete. They also built 50,000 kilometres of roads and were the first people to be really good at making
(5) _____ . The first bridge with a name was the Pons Fabricius, made of stone. They built it over the River Tiber in Rome in 62 BC and it is there today, two
(6) _____ years later.

8 Choose words from the box to label the pictures.

| metal | silver | plastic | wood | ~~glass~~ | card | paper | wool | gold |

1  **2** **3** **4** **5** **6**

glass_____ _____ _____ _____ _____ _____

9 Find and write eight materials.

p	a	p	e	r	y	w	u	a	p
l	s	c	o	s	i	l	v	e	r
a	k	t	a	m	a	t	l	c	b
s	a	o	d	r	f	e	q	o	w
t	w	t	n	f	d	a	i	l	o
i	g	o	l	d	u	a	h	t	o
c	n	m	o	v	m	e	t	a	l
d	c	p	o	d	t	r	t	g	k

1 g o l d   5 c _ _ _ _ _ _
2 s _ _ _ _ _ _ _ _ _   6 p _ _ _ _ _ _ _
3 p _ _ _ _ _ _ _ _ _   7 m _ _ _ _ _ _ _
4 w _ _ _ _ d   8 w _ _ _ _ l

10 Write the words.

1 A manmade material. We make it from oil. _plastic_____
2 An expensive white metal. _____
3 Animal hair. _____
4 Windows are made of this. It can break easily.
   _____
5 We get this material from sheep. _____

11 Look at the letters on the clock and write the words.

1 It's twenty-five past twelve.
   gold_____
2 It's ten to three.
   _____
3 It's twenty-five to one.
   _____
4 It's half past four.
   _____
5 It's quarter to eleven.
   _____
6 It's twenty to two.
   _____

Clock letters: ld, ver, at, wo, rd, sil, od, ca, tal, co, go, me

12 Read. Change one letter to write a new word.

face	Part of our body, on the front of our head.
race	A competition to see who's the fastest.
	Something we eat.
	Good, lovely.
	A number between eight and ten.
	My things, something I've got.
	A straight mark on a page or drawing.
	The opposite of *don't like*.
	Where do you … ?
	The opposite of *hate*.
	We do this with our body when we dance.
	Gold is … expensive than silver.
	The past of *wear*.
	The opposite of *play*.
	Part of a sentence.
	We get this material from trees.
	We get this material from sheep.
pool	Somewhere we can go to swim.

13 Now write the clues for this puzzle.

well	The opposite of 'badly'.
wall	
ball	
tall	
talk	
walk	

14 Find 8 mistakes in the text.

Glook's from a different world. He's doing a project about Earth and there are a lot of mistakes. Can you help him to correct his homework?

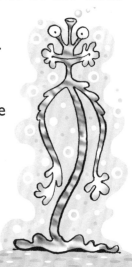

People on Earth use things which are made of different materials. Plastic, wood and (dictionaries) are all different materials. Bottles are made of glass or paper. Tables and chairs can be made of fog, cloud or metal. People on Earth like reading books, comics and volcanoes. These are made of card and wool. Earth people get wool from parrots. I'm going to visit Earth next November. I want to get a lovely big bracelet made of water. I can wear it when I go to parties.

15 Now write the text correctly.

People on Earth use things which are made of different materials. Plastic, wood and card are all different materials.

16 Match the rhyming words.

1 wool	a where ____	6 box	f bricks ____
2 near	b wood ____	7 six	g goes ____
3 stone	c pull _1_	8 wear	h socks _6_
4 pear	d here ____	9 nose	i ate ____
5 could	e bone ____	10 great	j hair ____

17 🔊 35 CD2 Listen, check and say.

18 Read and match.

Description of an object, how to use it and why.
- This is a house.
- It's made of brick.
- I can use it to put my things in.
- I can play in it.
- It's got lots of windows because I like looking at the garden.

Write it right

My dream house

1 My dream house is made	a food in it.
2 I can use it	b I like playing football.
3 I can cook my favourite	c of stone. `1`
4 It's got a big garden because	d so I can run around them.
5 There aren't any spiders in my house	e to sleep in.
6 There are ten rooms	f because I'm afraid of them.

19 Write about your dream house.

My dream house
My dream house is made of

20 Read and answer.

1 What was Brutus carrying in his bag? _The Baloney Stone._
2 What's the inside of Brutus's bag made of? _____
3 What did Brutus push? _____
4 Why's it dangerous to joke about Sirius? _____
5 What are the bowls made of? _____
6 What does Brutus want? _____

21 Read and order the text.

in his bag, but The Baloney Stone's safe ☐

because the inside's made of plastic. Diggory ☐

Brutus is carrying the computer [1]

the instructions. Brutus pushes the picture ☐

Cleopatra's treasure from her underwater palace. ☐

of the snake and a secret door opens. They ☐

find a lot of treasure behind the wall. It's ☐

understands the writing on the wall and reads ☐

? **Do you remember?**

1 Trees are made of _wood_ .
2 Scarves are made of _____ .
3 Gold and silver are precious _____ .
4 My friend is afraid _____ spiders.
5 A word which rhymes with 'gold' is '_____'.
6 Two words that rhyme with 'great' are '_____' and '_____'.

Can do

I can talk about materials.
I can talk about what things are made of.
I can write a description of a dream house.

☹ 😐 🙂
☹ 😐 🙂
☹ 😐 🙂

1 Look at the recycling facts. Read and write 'true' or 'false'.

> Recycling can't take the colours from plastics, so we can't use them for transparent containers.

> When you put plastic bottles in recycling banks, or even in your bin, always take the bottle top off. If you take the top off, it is easier to make them smaller.

> Every year in the United Kingdom, supermarkets give out 17,500,000,000 plastic bags. That is over 290 for every person in the UK.

> A lot of things are made from recycled plastic. These include polyethylene bags to put in bins, PVC floors and windows, video and CD boxes, furniture and waterproof clothes.

1 Take the top off bottles when you recycle them. true_____

2 We use recycled plastic for bin bags. _____

3 Recycling takes the colours from the plastic. _____

4 In the United Kingdom, supermarkets give out 17.5 million plastic bags a year. _____

5 PVC windows can be made of recycled plastic. _____

6 Supermarkets give people 50 bags a year. _____

2 What should we do? Put the information in the table.

> ~~Throw plastic toys away~~   Give toys to friends or playgroups
> Use plastic containers and bags again   Make containers into something else
> Throw plastic containers away   Use a bag if you don't need one
> Look for products made from recycled plastic   Use lots of plastic

Things we should do	Things we shouldn't do
	Throw plastic toys away

3 Write about what plastic things you use in your school and the changes you are going to make.

Plastic in my school

4 **Whose things are these?**

Listen and write a letter in each box. There is one example.

Sarah | E | Robert | ☐ | Emma | ☐ | Richard | ☐ | Katy | ☐ | Michael | ☐

A

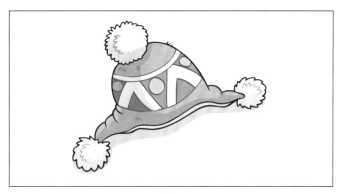

B

C

D

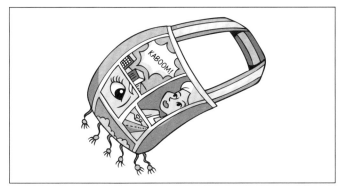

E

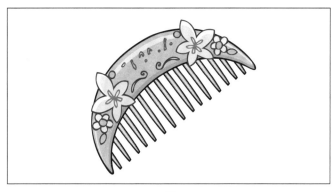

F

53

6 Senses

LOOK again **What … like?**

We use verb + *like* to describe things.

Affirmative	Negative (n't = not)	Question
It **looks like** a ball.	It **doesn't sound like** a car.	**What** does it **feel like**?
It **smells like** a lemon.	It **doesn't taste like** chocolate.	**What** does it **look like**?

1 Read and order the words.

1 blue cheese / smells / That / old / horrible.
   That old blue cheese smells horrible.

2 it's / rain. / going to / It / looks / like
   ----

3 mobile phone. / That / like / your / sounds
   ----

4 like? / does / this / toy mouse / What / feel
   ----

5 Her / cake / coffee. / tastes / like
   ----

6 look / like? / What / my picture / does
   ----

2 Correct the sentences.

1 Your mobile phone sound~~s~~ like a radio.

2 My sweater doesn't feels like fur.

3 That pen look likes a banana.

4 This biscuit don't taste like chocolate.

5 What does that cheese smells like?

6 I doesn't look like my dad.

3 Read and complete the email.

| hear | ~~Saturday~~ | feel | exciting | felt | quickly | shouting |

Hi Frank,

How was your weekend? I had a really good one because on (1) _Saturday_ we went to a new theme park. It's really (2) ------------ and has got lots of things to do. Can you see the picture of the rollercoaster? It's amazing! That's me (3) ----------- loudly. I thought it looked dangerous, but I didn't (4) ----------- afraid. It sounded very loud, though – I couldn't (5) ----------- anything.

I also went on a big wheel. You sit in a chair and it goes round and round very (6) ------------ . At first I felt excited, but then I felt sick. When I got off I didn't feel very well. I (7) ----------- ill, but I liked it.

Let's speak soon.

Richard

54

4 How do they look? Write the answers.

1 <u>She looks pleased.</u>

2 _____

3 _____

4 _____

5 _____

6 _____

5 Read. What are they?

1 It looks like an apple, but it isn't round. It's green and yellow. What is it? <u>a pear</u>

2 It looks like a bean, but it isn't. It's green, small and round. What is it? _____

3 It's a fruit and it tastes like a lime, but it isn't green. It's yellow. What is it? _____

4 It's a hot drink. Some people have it with sugar and milk. It sometimes looks like coffee, but it doesn't taste like coffee. What is it? _____

5 They sometimes taste like burgers. They are long and thin. What are they? _____

6 This sounds like a lion, but it isn't. It's got orange fur and black stripes. What is it? _____

6 Senses quiz. Read and answer.

1 Which part of the body do we use to taste? <u>Our tongue.</u>

2 Which part of the body do we use to smell? _____

3 Which parts of the body do we use to see? _____

4 Which parts of the body do we use to hear? _____

5 Which parts of the body can we use to touch things? _____

6 What are your favourite sounds? _____

7 What smells make you hungry? _____

8 Which of your senses do you think is the strongest? _____

7 Choose words from the box to label the pictures.

| flour | knife | salt | fork | ~~pepper~~ | spoon | plate | pizza |

1 **2** **3** **4** **5** **6**

pepper _____ _____ _____ _____ _____ _____

8 Look and find the words.

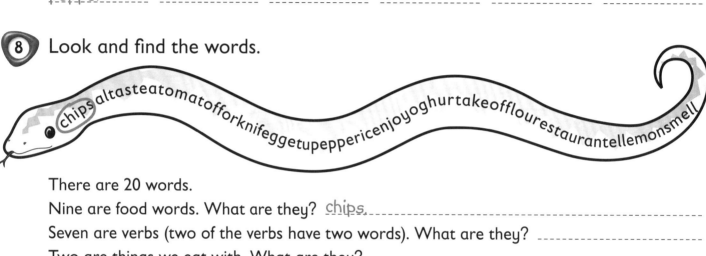

chipsaltasteatomatofforknifeggetupeppericenjoyoghurtakeofflourestaurantellemonsmell

There are 20 words.
Nine are food words. What are they? chips, _____
Seven are verbs (two of the verbs have two words). What are they? _____
Two are things we eat with. What are they? _____
One is a preposition. What is it? _____
One is somewhere we go to eat. What is it? _____

9 Read and write the answers in the puzzle.

1 We put this on our food. It's black or white. ~~pepper~~ _____
2 We use this with a knife when we eat. _____
3 We use this in cooking. It's white. We get it
   from the sea or the ground. _____
4 Famous Italian food. _____
5 We put our food on this when we
   eat. _____
6 Bread is made of this. _____
7 We use this to cut meat. _____
8 We use this to eat ice cream. _____

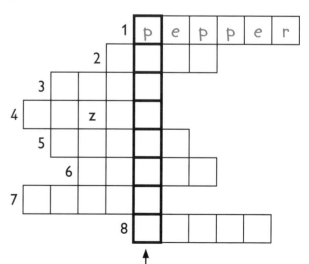

1 | p | e | p | p | e | r
2
3
4 | | z
5
6
7
8

What's the mystery vegetable? _____

10 Read and complete the text.

900	metres	cook	meal	cheese	largest	flour
made	Italy	~~people~~	pizzas	top	taste	

The (1) people _____ from Naples (Napoli) in (2) _____
were the first to make (3) _____ . Their pizzas are
(4) _____ of a bread base, with (5) _____ , tomato
and olives on top. Pizzas are people's favourite (6) _____
all over the world, not only in Italy, because they (7) _____
delicious. Some pizzas can have extra things on (8) _____ .
They can have thicker bases and sometimes the (9) _____
can fold the pizza in half and fill it with more cheese and things. They
cook pizzas in an oven. The (10) _____ pizza ever made was in South Africa in 1990. It was
enormous! It was 37.4 (11) _____ across and was made with 500 kg of (12) _____ ,
800 kg of cheese and (13) _____ kg of tomatoes. Amazing!

ITALY
Naples

11 Read and order the text.

	programmes. When his family came home, it looked like the kitchen was on
	were out. He decided to cook sausages and potatoes. He turned on the
1	Tom's 14. Last Saturday he decided to make lunch for his family while they
	into the hot water. He did this because sugar looks like salt and he didn't read
6	the label on the box. Then he went into the living room to watch TV while he
	to turn on the clock. Then he started to cook the potatoes, but he put sugar
	was waiting for the food to cook and started to watch one of his favourite
9	fire. When they opened the oven, the sausages looked small and black. The
	potatoes were OK, but they tasted sweet. Tom's mum said he invented sweet potatoes!
	oven and when it felt hot, he put the sausages inside, but he forgot

12 Write the words in the columns.

~~Daisy~~   ~~Lucy~~   scar<u>f</u>   chip<u>s</u>   amazing   dangerou<u>s</u>
word<u>s</u>   animal<u>s</u>   <u>c</u>entre   chee<u>s</u>e   <u>s</u>mell   potatoe<u>s</u>

s (plant<u>s</u>)	z (leg<u>s</u>)
Lucy	Daisy

13 [11 CD3] Listen, check and say.

14 Read this diamante poem and answer the questions.

Summer
Hot,   dry
Playing, swimming, reading
Sun,   beach,   snow,   wind
Studying, sleeping, raining
Cold,   wet
Winter

Poems
Diamante poems always have seven lines and a specific number of words per line, in this order: one, two, three, four, three, two, one. They use the same kinds of words and they are always in two halves.

Write it right

1 What's it about? It's about summer and

2 How does it make you feel?

15 Look at the poem again and complete the table.

Line 1.   1   word   noun
Line 2. __ words   _____
Line 3. __ words   action verbs
Line 4. __ words   _____
Line 5. __ words   _____
Line 6. __ words   _____
Line 7. __ word   _____

16 Write your diamante poem.

58

17 Read and answer.

1 Where does Brutus fall? <u>He falls into a snake bowl.</u>
2 What's inside the snake bowl?
----
3 What does Diggory use to get Brutus out?
----
4 Who's got The Baloney Stone now? ----------------
5 What is the dog? --------------------------------
6 Who does Brutus push into the snake bowl?
----

18 Correct the sentences.

1 At first, Brutus thought that the animals felt like a mouse.
<u>At first, Brutus thought that the animals felt like a spider.</u>
2 The dangerous ancient trap is called a snake plate.
----
3 Brutus loves spiders.
----
4 The snake didn't wake up.
----
5 Diggory used his scarf to help Brutus out of the snake bowl.
----
6 Brutus thought the dog was the window.

? **Do you remember?**

1 A lemon sometimes <u>looks</u> like a lime.
2 Pizza doesn't smell ----------------- spaghetti.
3 You need a spoon and a ----------------- to mix salad.
4 You need an ----------------- to cook pizza.
5 Two words which end with 's' (as in 'plant<u>s</u>') are -----------------
and ----------------- .
6 A diamante poem has ----------------- lines.

Can do   I can talk about the five senses.
                 I can plan a party.
                 I can write a poem.

59

1 Read the text. What does it say? Write it correctly.

Cna yuo undretsnad waht tihs snetnece syas? Teh ltteres aer mexid so wehn yuo look at ti, it si dfificult ot undretsnad. Bceause yruo brian is vrey clveer, ti cna reda it.

<u>Can</u> _____

_____

_____

2 Look at the pictures. What can you see?

1 Can you read any words in a and b? _____

2 What are they? _____ _____ _____

3 Which line looks longer, c or d? _____

4 Now measure the two lines. What do you find out? _____

5 Which animal does it look like in e?

_____

6 Now turn the picture round. Can you see a different animal? What is it?

_____

3 Make your optical illusion.

- Colour the squares: black–white–black–white …

- Don't colour the grey lines.

What can you see? _____

_____

_____

4 Write about your favourite optical illusion.

My favourite optical illusion

5 **Look at the picture and read the story. Write some words to complete the sentences about the story. You can use 1, 2, 3 or 4 words.**

Helen is twelve and she's got a brother called William, who's six. Last Saturday Helen's dad took them to an art museum in the city centre. They were very pleased. There was a show of modern art by a famous artist and the museum was full of people. Helen was standing in front of a painting, looking at it when William said, 'This looks like a really big pizza with small tomatoes and olives on it.'

Helen said, 'You don't understand modern art, William. This is a great painting that shows us that life is beautiful, but difficult.' Helen's dad laughed and said, 'I think William understands modern art better than you, Helen. Look!' Helen's dad pointed and Helen saw the title of the painting. It was called 'Pizza with tomatoes and olives'.

Example

Helen's brother is six .... years old.

Questions

1 Helen's got .... called William.

2 Last Saturday Helen and William .... art museum with their father.

3 The show was by a famous artist and there were a lot of .... at the museum.

4 One painting .... like a really big pizza.

5 Helen's dad read the title of the ....

Review Units  5 and 6

 1 Read the story. Choose words from the box to complete the sentences.

pizza	flour	sounded	plastic	like	felt	were	~~competition~~	touch
film	made							

Friendly

Last November Sue won an important art (1) __competition__ for her painting *Modern Girl*, which she said looked (2) ------------------ Jenny. The prize was a meal for two in Luigi's, the town's best Italian restaurant.

Sue invited Jenny to have lunch with her. Jenny felt very pleased. She bought a new dress which was (3) ------------------ of bright yellow wool. She wore it with a big brown (4) ------------------ belt and a dark brown jacket. She looked like a 'Modern Girl' and she (5) ------------------ like a film star. The two friends felt hungry when they arrived at the restaurant. The waiter put their (6) ------------------ on the table and they agreed it smelled like the best in the world. When they were eating it, they said it tasted like nothing on Earth – it was delicious. After the pizza, Luigi came out of the kitchen and carefully put the second course on the table. It was his most famous sweet, 'Banana and Chocolate Surprise'. Sue and Jenny felt very surprised. It looked just like Jenny's clothes!

2 Choose a title for this episode of *Friendly*.

   a) The cook's famous clothes   b) A sweet dress   c) Jenny looks like a pear

3 Find the odd one out.

1 silver   metal   gold   (plastic)
   Plastic isn't a metal. ------------------

2 salt   olives   wool   pepper
   ----

3 eyes   feel   taste   smell
   ----

4 spoon   bracelet   knife   fork
   ----

5 wool   hair   stone   fur
   ----

6 wood   paper   card   glass
   ----

4 Complete the sentences. Count and write the letters.

1 Her mobile phone _sounds_ like a baby laughing.

2 We've got five senses. They are sight, hearing, touch, smell and _____ .

3 We use a _____ to cut meat.

4 _____ is a material we get from sheep.

5 The opposite of strong is _____ .

6 What does that cloud look _____ ?

7 We hear with our _____ .

8 We use a _____ to eat soup.

9 _____ is an expensive white metal.

10 Knives and forks can be made of metal or _____ .

11 _____ is a material we get from trees.

12 What's your bracelet _____ of? Metal.

13 We feel _____ if we don't drink.

14 We serve food on a _____ .

6

5 Now complete the crossword. Write the message.

1	2	3	4	5	1
		U			

6	7	8	9		10	3	4
						U		!

6 Quiz time!

1 What is Alvin's spider made of?
Alvin's spider is made of fur.
_____

2 What is Arsenault's house made of?
_____

3 What is celluloid used for?
_____

4 What smells like Alvin's socks?
_____

5 What does Luigi's Italian restaurant make? _____

6 What does the painting *Mae West* look like? _____

7 Write questions for your quiz in your notebook.

7 Natural world

LOOK again | Should

We use *should* to give and ask for help or advice.

Affirmative	Negative (n't = not)	Question
I **should look after** the countryside.	You **shouldn't throw** rubbish on the ground.	**Should** he **help** his mum in the garden?
She **should tidy up** her room.	We **shouldn't forget** that we only have one world.	**Should** they **drive** a big car?

1 Read and match.

1 What should you wear if you go for a long walk?	You should wear a coat and scarf.
2 What should you wear outdoors on a sunny day?	You should stop and look both ways.
3 What should you wear when it's very cold?	1 You should wear strong shoes.
4 Who should you ask if you get lost in a big city?	To protect your skin from the sun.
5 What should you do when you cross the road?	You should ask a police officer.
6 Why should you use sun cream?	You should wear a hat.

2 Think and write 'should' or 'shouldn't'.

1 It's a sunny day and Emma's at the beach. She _should_ wear a hat.
2 Michael's got a headache. He _____ watch TV.
3 Betty's got a terrible toothache. She _____ go to the dentist.
4 David wants to cross the road. He _____ stop and look both ways first.
5 Katy _____ eat chocolate because she's got a stomach-ache.
6 Harry's got an important exam tomorrow, so he _____ study this afternoon.

3 Correct the sentences.

1 We've should look after the countryside. _We should look after the countryside._
2 We should to walk on the paths. _____
3 We should drop our rubbish. _____
4 We always should use bins. _____
5 We shouldn't of play with animals in fields. _____
6 We's shouldn't drink water from rivers. _____

4 Match the problems with the correct advice.

 **Pamela's Problem Page**

1.
Dear Pamela,
I saw my friend copying in an exam. What should I do?

2.
Dear Pamela,
I'm having real problems with Maths at school. What should I do?

3.
Dear Pamela,
My friends are going to go to the cinema on Saturday, but my parents say I can't go. What should I do?

4.
Dear Pamela,
I want to have a dog for my birthday, but my mum and dad say I can't have one. What should I do?

5.
Dear Pamela,
I want to learn to climb, but I don't live near the mountains. What should I do?

6.
Dear Pamela,
I don't like vegetables, but my mum says I have to eat carrots and peas every day. I hate dinner time. What should I do?

a.
Why don't you talk to them and ask to go to see the film another day? You should ask them to come with you.

b.
If you don't understand something, you should always talk to your teacher. She'll be pleased to help you.

c.
You should look on the internet for a climbing club in your nearest city. You can climb up special climbing walls.

d.
You should ask your mum if you can try a different vegetable every day until you find some that you like.

e.
It's important to remember if your parents say no, they know why. Ask them to talk to you about it.

f.
You should talk to your friend and tell him not to do it again. If that doesn't work, then tell your teacher.

1 [f]   2 [ ]   3 [ ]   4 [ ]   5 [ ]   6 [ ]

 5 Think and write advice.

1 Someone who's going to the beach on a hot day.
2 Someone who's got a headache.
3 Someone who wants to learn English.
4 Someone who wants to try a new hobby.
5 Someone who wants to learn more about the past.
6 Someone who is always fighting with their brother.

1   You should take a hat and sun cream. You shouldn't lie in the sun all day.

6 Answer the questions.

1 Do your friends talk to you when they have a problem? _____
2 Do you help your friends? _____
3 Do you think you should always keep secrets? _____
4 Who do you talk to when you have a problem? _____
5 What are the biggest problems for you and your friends? _____
6 When should you tell your teacher about a problem? _____

7 Choose words from the box to label the pictures.

> Lehmann's poison frog   Purple spotted butterfly   ~~Mountain zebra~~
> Siberian tiger   Nine-spotted ladybug beetle

Mountain zebra _____ _____ _____ _____ _____

8 Sort and write the words.

1 sigwn   wings _____
2 erttflbyu _____
3 tisnce _____

4 opst _____
5 pitser _____
6 ufr _____

7 iatl _____
8 dboy _____
9 tbeele _____

9 Now match the words with the definitions.

1 beetle _____ This insect has got two hard wings and two soft wings.
2 _____ The hair an animal has on its body.
3 _____ The parts of an insect or animal which it uses to fly.
4 _____ Lions, tigers, elephants and mice all have one of these. It comes out of the back part of their bodies.
5 _____ The part of an animal or insect which has the arms and legs on it.
6 _____ An insect with two beautiful wings, six legs and two antennae.
7 _____ A small animal with a body, six legs and two eyes.
8 _____ A small coloured circle on a different colour.
9 _____ An area between two lines which is a different colour.

10 Write the words in the table.

> ~~through~~   ~~become~~   ~~funny~~   ~~spot~~   extinction   recycle   wing   into   appear
> extinct   spotted   over   across   explore   stripe   warm

adjectives	verbs	prepositions	nouns
funny _____ _____	become _____ _____	through _____ _____	spot _____ _____
_____ _____	_____ _____	_____ _____	_____ _____

11 Match the pictures of endangered animals with the words.

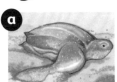 a
 b
 c
 d

1 Leatherback turtle [a]
2 Orang-utan [ ]
3 White rhino [ ]
4 Iberian lynx [ ]
5 Whale [ ]
6 Giant panda [ ]
7 Bearded vulture [ ]
8 Bat [ ]

 e
 f
 g
 h

12 Now find out one fact about each of the endangered animals in Activity 11.

Leatherback turtles live in the Pacific Ocean.

13 Now make a quiz for your friends.

Endangered animals quiz
1 Where do leatherback turtles live?

14 Read and order the story.

	'What is your question?' the teacher asked.
	The old man said, 'I don't know either. Here are your two pounds!'
1	One day a very clever teacher went to a small village in the country.
	The teacher was happy with the old man's idea because he was very clever.
	The teacher thought for a long time, but he didn't know the answer.
	'What animal has got three heads, two wings and one leg?' the old man asked.
	He was talking to the people there when an old man spoke to him: 'I have a question for you. If you can't answer my question, you give me ten pounds. Then you ask me a question. If I can't answer it, I give you two pounds.'
	After 30 minutes thinking, he gave the old man his ten pounds and said, 'I'm sorry. I don't know the answer. What is it?'

15 Write the opposites.

| white | ~~old~~ | long | past | cold | night | strong | last |

1 young and _old_
2 hot and _____
3 black and _____
4 day and _____

5 short and _____
6 weak and _____
7 present and _____
8 first and _____

16 🎵 22 CD3 Listen, check and say.

17 Read and number the parts of the letter.

1 — 13 West Street
Chester
15 March 2015

Dear Mrs Smith,

I'm writing to ask you for information about recycling bins at our school.

  In my class we think we should recycle all paper and bottles. There are some questions I'd like to ask. Can you bring some bins to our school, please? Also, when can I come to talk to you?

  Thank you very much.
Yours sincerely,
Emily Wood

Writing a letter
A polite letter should have:
1 Your address
2 Today's date
3 The name of the person who you're writing to
4 The reason why you're writing
5 An end
6 Your name

Write it right

18 Now write a letter to Mrs Green about recycling. Ask her for information about the recycling bins.

_____
_____
_____

Dear Mrs Green, _____
_____
_____
_____
_____
_____
_____
_____

19 Read and answer.

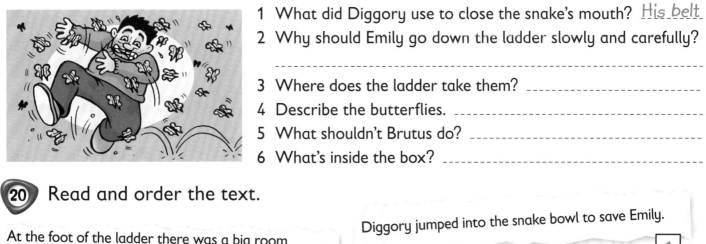

1 What did Diggory use to close the snake's mouth? *His belt*
2 Why should Emily go down the ladder slowly and carefully?
----
3 Where does the ladder take them? _____
4 Describe the butterflies. _____
5 What shouldn't Brutus do? _____
6 What's inside the box? _____

20 Read and order the text.

At the foot of the ladder there was a big room full of butterflies. ☐

Thousands of butterflies flew off the walls to protect their young. ☐

There was a ladder under the door. They climbed slowly and carefully down it. ☐

Then he put his belt round the snake's mouth so it couldn't bite them. ☐

Diggory jumped into the snake bowl to save Emily. 1

The box was full of striped insects, so Brutus dropped it. ☐

Diggory knew how to get out. He opened a secret door. ☐

When Diggory and Emily were looking at the butterflies, Brutus opened a box. ☐

The room was the famous butterfly room of Queen Hetepheres. ☐

? Do you remember?

1 I've got a problem. What *should* _____ I do?
2 You _____ throw rubbish on the floor. Put it in a bin.
3 The Lost Ladybug Project asks people to take _____ of these endangered beetles.
4 Two endangered animals which have _____ are tigers and zebras.
5 'Hot' and '_____' are opposites.
6 You should write your _____ in the top right corner of a letter.

Can do
I can describe insects and animals.
I can talk about things we should or shouldn't do.
I can write a letter.

☹ 😐 🙂
☹ 😐 🙂
☹ 😐 🙂

Science | Extinction

1 Read the factfile and complete the text.

Name	When it died	Where	Description	Interesting facts
Archaeopteryx	About 150 million years ago	Germany in Europe	Length – 30 cm long from beak to tail Wings – 0.5 m across Weight – 300–500 grams	The Archaeopteryx was the first animal to fly. It ate meat.

The (1) _Archaeopteryx_ was a dinosaur which lived about one hundred and
(2) ----------------- million years ago. It lived in (3) ----------------- in
Europe. It was (4) ----------------- cm long and had (5) -----------------
which were 50 centimetres across. It weighed between (6) -----------------
hundred and five (7) ----------------- grams. The Archaeopteryx was the
first (8) ----------------- to fly. Its favourite food was (9) ----------------- .

2 Now read and write about the Diplodocus.

Name	When it died	Where	Description	Interesting facts
Diplodocus	About 145–155 million years ago	There are a lot of Diplodocus bones in the Rocky Mountains in the USA.	Length – 27 m long Height – 5 m tall Weight – 10–20 tons	Diplodocus was enormous. It had an 8 m long neck and a 14 m long tail. Its head was not more than 60 cm long. Its front legs were shorter than its back legs, and all legs had feet like an elephant's. It was a herbivore and ate leaves from trees.

The Diplodocus was an enormous dinosaur
which lived

(3) **Listen and draw lines. There is one example.**

Betty   Harry   Richard   George

Katy   Holly   Sarah

8 World of sport

LOOK again | **Present perfect**

We use the *present perfect* to talk and write about things we did and do.

Affirmative	Negative (n't = not)	Question
I**'ve played** tennis.	You **haven't played** volleyball.	**Has** he **played** basketball?
She**'s been** skiing.	We **haven't been** swimming.	**Have** they **been** running?

1 Are these verbs regular or irregular? Write 'R' or 'I'.

arrive _R_   lose _I_   believe ____   make ____   stop ____   play ____

meet ____   catch ____   jump ____   win ____   finish ____   wash ____

2 Make negative sentences.

1 I've sailed from England to Ireland.
   I haven't sailed from England to Ireland.

2 She's won a prize.
   ----

3 They've played basketball.
   ----

4 He's climbed the highest mountain.
   ----

5 You've won the game.
   ----

6 We've made a kite.
   ----

3 Match the pictures with the text.

It's the first time she's played badminton! ☐

It's the first time he's won a prize. [1]

I've never made a cake before. ☐

This is the first time you've worked in a restaurant, isn't it? ☐

Is this the first time they've washed the car? ☐

We've never been ice skating before. ☐

4 Answer the questions.

1 What's the third letter in **heard**? _a_
2 What's the second letter in **climbed**? _ _ _ _
3 What's the fifth letter in **stopped**? _ _ _ _
4 What's the first letter in **hockey**? _ _ _ _
5 What's the third letter in **skated**? _ _ _ _
6 What's the first letter in **badminton**? _ _ _ _
7 What's the sixth letter in **started**? _ _ _ _
8 What's the fourth letter in **football**? _ _ _ _
What's the word? _ _ _ _ _ _ _ _ _ _ _ _ _ _ _ _ _ _

5 Now make your word puzzle.

1 What's the seventh letter in **basketball**?
2 What's the first letter in **appeared**?

6 Write the correct form of the verbs in the email.

Hi Joe,

I'm writing to tell you about the things I've
(1) _done_ (do) in the last month or two. We haven't
(2) _ _ _ _ _ _ _ _ _ _ _ (talk) for two months. I'm sorry, but
I've been really busy. I've (3) _ _ _ _ _ _ _ _ _ _ _ (study) a lot
because I've got exams next week, and at last I've
(4) _ _ _ _ _ _ _ _ _ _ _ (finish) the book which you gave me
for my birthday. It was really interesting.

Let me tell you what's (5) _ _ _ _ _ _ _ _ _ _ _ (happen)
at the sports club. You know that I was in the hockey
team, don't you? Well, I've (6) _ _ _ _ _ _ _ _ _ _ _ (decide)
to change sports. I've (7) _ _ _ _ _ _ _ _ _ _ _ (stop) playing
hockey and now I've (8) _ _ _ _ _ _ _ _ _ _ _ (start) racing my
bike. It's very difficult, but I like it. I've (9) _ _ _ _ _ _ _ _ _ _ _
(race) twice, and I finished fifth and ninth. Not bad, really.
Look at the photo. I'm in it!
Have you ever (10) _ _ _ _ _ _ _ _ _ _ _ (win) a race?
Write soon!

7 Look at the pictures. Write the questions.

What have they
done?

_ _ _ _ _ _ _ _ _ _ _ _ _ _ _ _ _ _
_ _ _ _ _ _ _ _ _ _ _ _ _ _ _ _ _ _

_ _ _ _ _ _ _ _ _ _ _ _ _ _ _ _ _ _
_ _ _ _ _ _ _ _ _ _ _ _ _ _ _ _ _ _

_ _ _ _ _ _ _ _ _ _ _ _ _ _ _ _ _ _
_ _ _ _ _ _ _ _ _ _ _ _ _ _ _ _ _ _

8 Now answer the questions.

1 _They've arrived in London._
2 _
3 _
4 _
5 _
6 _

9 Choose words from the box to label the pictures.

| golf | sledging | volleyball | athletics | ~~skiing~~ | snowboarding | cycling | tennis |

1 **2** **3** **4** **5** **6**

skiing_____ _____ _____ _____ _____ _____

10 Write the seasons.

1 This is the hottest season. summer_____

2 In this season all the new flowers start growing. _____

3 This is the season when trees lose their leaves. _____

4 This is the coldest season. This season comes after the autumn. _____

11 Write the sports words in the table.

| ~~soccer~~ | table tennis | sailing | ice skating | basketball | sledging |
| cycling | horse-riding | skiing | tennis | ice hockey | athletics |

winter sports	ball sports	other sports
_____	soccer_____	_____
_____	_____	_____
_____	_____	_____
_____	_____	_____

12 What are the sports? Write the words in the puzzle.

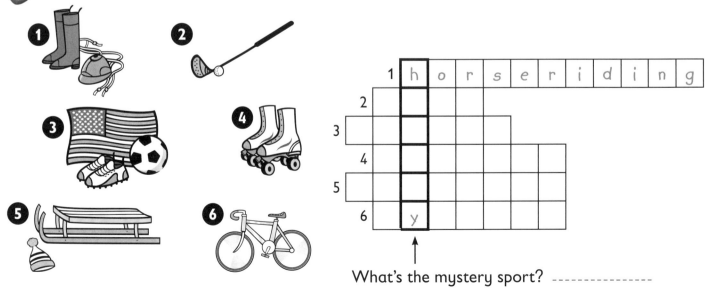

	1	h	o	r	s	e	r	i	d	i	n	g
2						
3					
4					
5					
6		y			

What's the mystery sport? _____

13 Write the sports.

| snowboarding | ~~table tennis~~ | sailing | golf | basketball | waterskiing |

1 You play inside with a small ball, two bats and a table. _table tennis_

2 This is a team game. Each team has five players. In this sport you can bounce, throw and catch the big ball. ----------------

3 You do this sport on mountains when there is snow. You have to stand up to do it. ----------------

4 You do this sport on water. You need a boat. ----------------

5 You can do this on the sea or on a lake. You stand up and a boat pulls you. ----------------

6 This is not a team game and you have to play outside. The players hit a very small ball around a course with 18 holes. ----------------

14 Now write definitions for six more sports.

1 You usually do this sport outside. You need a bicycle.

15 Read and complete the table.

Three friends live in houses next to each other in Ice Road and they have made a snowman. Where does each friend live? What has each child brought to put on the snowman?

Robert lives at number 3. He didn't bring a carrot for the snowman's nose. Sally brought a scarf for the snowman. Richard doesn't live next to Robert. One of the boys brought a hat for the snowman.

Name			Robert
House number			
Thing for the snowman			

16 Choose the story. Then draw your snowman in your notebook.

Last weekend it was very cold and it snowed a lot. We went outside to play in the **park / forest / garden**. First we **played / jumped / sledged** in the snow. Then we decided to make a **big / small / tall / fat / funny / thin** snowman.

When we finished making it, we gave it a **carrot / banana / pear** for a nose and some **leaves / rocks / stones** for a mouth. Then we put an old **brown / red / purple** hat on its head and a long **spotted / striped** scarf round its neck. The scarf was **blue and green / pink and purple / red and yellow**. Finally we put two **orange / grey / black** gloves on sticks and put them into its body. The gloves were made of **leather / wool / rubber**. Our snowman looked **happy / sad / surprised / angry / amazing**. We called it ---------------- .

17 Match the rhyming words.

1 wore   a through ____   7 laughed   g should ____
2 said   b bought ____   8 heard   h child ____
3 skated   c made ____   9 won   i belt ____
4 flew   d four _1_   10 spelt   j craft _7_
5 played   e head ____   11 stood   k word ____
6 caught   f waited ____   12 smiled   l done ____

18 🎵 **34 CD3** Listen, check and say.

19 Find and circle information about what, when, where and why. Make four circles in total.

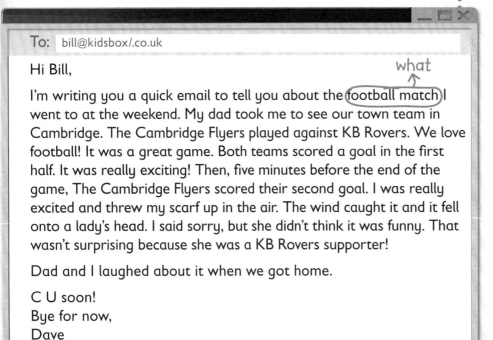

To: bill@kidsbox/.co.uk

Hi Bill,

what ↑

I'm writing you a quick email to tell you about the (football match) I went to at the weekend. My dad took me to see our town team in Cambridge. The Cambridge Flyers played against KB Rovers. We love football! It was a great game. Both teams scored a goal in the first half. It was really exciting! Then, five minutes before the end of the game, The Cambridge Flyers scored their second goal. I was really excited and threw my scarf up in the air. The wind caught it and it fell onto a lady's head. I said sorry, but she didn't think it was funny. That wasn't surprising because she was a KB Rovers supporter!

Dad and I laughed about it when we got home.

C U soon!
Bye for now,
Dave

Emails
• An email to a friend is normally very friendly.
• You need to write your friend's email address in the box at the top.
• You don't need to write your address or the date.
• You can start your email saying 'Hi' or 'Hello'.
• To make your email interesting, include information about what, when, where and why.
• You can finish your email saying 'All the best' or 'Bye for now'.

Write it right

20 Now write your email about something that happened at the weekend.

Hi _____ ,
I'm writing you a quick email _____
_____
_____
_____
_____
_____

21 Read and answer.

1 Why shouldn't Brutus open his mouth? _The butterflies are dangerous._
2 Has Diggory ever used the new door? _____
3 Which sports did the Ancient Egyptians invent? _____
4 Where did Diggory send the email from? _____
5 What does the Ancient Story of Sirius say? _____
_____

22 Who said it? Read and match.

1  **2**  **3**  **4**

a They've painted sports on these walls. `3`

b It's the first time anyone's used this door. ☐

c I've waited for this moment all my life. ☐

d Now what have you done? ☐

e I haven't touched anything. ☐

f You're the 'treasure' now, Brutus! ☐

? Do you remember?

1 Have you ever _been_ to Egypt?
2 He's _____ the race. Now he can celebrate!
3 They haven't _____ badminton before.
4 _____ is the season which comes after spring.
5 One word which rhymes with 'said' is _____ .
6 You can say '_____ for now' at the end of an email to a friend.

Can do

I can talk about things I have done.
I can talk about different sports.
I can write an email.

1 Choose words from the box to complete the text.

| football | countries | always | ~~four~~ | started | well | athletes | swimming |

There are Paralympic Games every (1) _four_ years. Paralympic Games are
(2) _____ in the same city as the full Olympic Games. They are for (3) _____
who have a disability. Disability means they have problems doing some things. Some athletes
can't see (4) _____ or can't see at all and others can't walk. The Paralympic Games
(5) _____ in Rome in 1960 and in each Paralympics there are more (6) _____ and
more athletes competing.

2 Invent a sport for the next Olympics.

Write your ideas on the mind map.

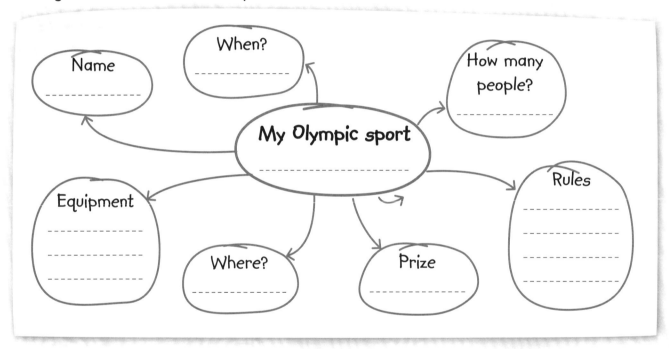

3 Now use the information in your mind map to write a letter to the Olympic
Committee telling them about your sport.

Dear Olympic Committee,
I'm writing to tell you about my new sport. I would like it to be in the
next Olympic Games. It's called

Read the text. Choose the right words and write them on the lines.

Winter sports

Example Winter sports is the name we give to sports which...............
1   people do on snow. .... sports are very popular
2   in countries where it is cold in .... winter. One of
3   the most popular sports is skiing. There .... three
4   kinds of .... at the Olympic Games today. One
5   is downhill skiing, where .... race down a hill. In
6   another kind, people .... across the countryside.
7   They can race up to fifty kilometres. The ....
8   kind is ski jumping which is very .... Skating,
9   snowboarding and sledging are just some .... the
        other winter sports. At the Winter Olympic Games there are
10   .... than ten different sports.

Example who   when   which
1   This   That   These
2   the   a   those
3   is   are   was
4   skied   skiing   skying
5   person   people   persons
6   racing   race   races
7   three   third   thirty
8   excited   excites   exciting
9   of   at   over
10 most   much   more

Review Units  7 and 8

1 Read the story. Choose a word from the box. Write the correct word next to numbers 1–6.

| taking | was | ride | snowman | ~~ever~~ | were | done | skis | coming |
| sledge | are | | | | | | | |

Friendly

Have you (1) _ever_ been skiing? This is what happened to Jim and Sally when they went last winter.

Last January the five friends went skiing with the school. On the first day, Sue, Peter and Jenny decided that it was too dangerous for them, so they chose a sledge and found somewhere nice and quiet at the bottom of the mountain to (2) _____ on it. Jim and Sally got their skis and went quickly to the ski lift which was taking the other skiers to the top of the mountain. It was Sally's first time on a ski lift, but Jim told her it was easy and she felt really excited. They sat on the thin metal seat, held the long piece of metal which was between them and the lift started. When they (3) _____ going up the mountain, Sally fell off. She fell onto her face and stomach with her skis crossed behind her and she couldn't move. The other skiers, who were coming up on the lift behind her, couldn't stop and fell off too. Sally took her (4) _____ off to move away, but she dropped them and they fell quickly down the mountain.

Sue, Peter and Jenny, who were sledging happily at the bottom of the mountain, suddenly saw Sally's skis coming, but they couldn't do anything and the skis hit their (5) _____ . They all fell off into the snow.

On the second day, the friends decided to do something safer. They made a (6) _____ !

2 Choose a title for this episode of *Friendly*.

a) Snow feels cold   b) Snowy disaster!   c) Summer holidays

3 Match the questions with the answers.

1	What can you catch but not throw?			A watchdog.
2	Waiter! Waiter! What's this fly doing on my ice cream?			Because 7 ate 9.
3	Where do horses go when they feel ill?			I think it's skiing, sir.
4	What's worse than finding an insect in your apple?		1	A cold.
5	What goes 'Tick tock woof tick tock woof'?			To a horspital.
6	Why was 10 afraid of 7?			Finding only half an insect in your apple.

80

4 Complete the sentences. Count and write the letters.

1 Snowboarding isn't easy. It's quite _difficult_ . **9**

2 Have you _____ won a prize? No, never. ☐

3 When a plant or animal species doesn't exist any more, it's _____ . ☐

4 He's _____ his homework, so now he can watch TV. ☐

5 When something's got spots, it's _____ . ☐

6 What _____ they done? They've washed the car. ☐

7 When we have a picnic, we _____ pick our rubbish up. ☐

8 The Diplodocus is an extinct _____ . ☐

9 Animals that fly need two _____ . ☐

10 He's the winner. He's _____ higher than the other jumpers. ☐

11 The Olympic _____ is a sports competition which is every four years. ☐

12 Zebras have got black and white _____ on their fur. ☐

13 Animal hair is called _____ . ☐

14 You play _____ on grass, hitting a small ball into holes with a long stick. ☐

5 Now complete the crossword. Write the message.

| d | i | ⁴f | f | i | c | u | l | t |

| 1 | 2 | 3 | 1 | | 4 | 2 | 5 | 6 |
| ☐ | ☐ | ☐ | ☐ | | f | ☐ | ☐ | ☐ |

6 Quiz time!

1 What should people do with their rubbish?
They should _____

2 What has two soft and two hard wings?
_____

3 Why did the dinosaurs become extinct?
_____

4 How many races has Alvin won?
_____

5 When do people go skiing?
_____

6 Where were the 2004 Olympics?
_____

7 Write questions for your quiz in your notebook.

Respect in the classroom

1 Read and choose the answer.

How good a student are you?

1 How often do you have breakfast before you go to school?

a never   **b** sometimes   **c** always

2 What time do you go to bed on school days?

a after 11 o'clock
b at about ten o'clock
c before ten o'clock

3 When do you prepare your school bag?

a before I go to bed
b I don't prepare it
c before I leave the house

4 How often do you talk to your friends during lessons?

a never   **b** sometimes   **c** always

5 Is it funny to take your friend's pencil case during the lesson?

a Yes   **b** I don't know   **c** No

6 When do you normally arrive for your lessons?

a when you want to
b after the lesson starts
c before the lesson starts

2 Write a class contract.

1 We must arrive on time.
2
3
4
5
6 When we do all these things correctly, we can:
   •
   •

Class Contract

Read and order the text.

	his car. Fire fighters had to cut the car door
	accident. The police officers drove Harry
	much better. He's going to leave
	had a bad car accident. His car hit a
	the hospital a team of doctors and
	officers phoned the hospital and
	Harry's life. Now, two weeks later, Harry is
	lorry and he couldn't get out of
	told the nurses about Harry and his
	to help stop the traffic. At
	to the hospital with the ambulance
	nurses worked together to save
1	Last week William's dad, Harry,
	hospital and go home to his family.
	and pull Harry out. Police

 Write a letter to thank the fire fighters.

Imagine that you are William. Write a letter to say thank you to the fire fighters, police officers and doctors who saved your dad's life. Use these words to help you.

two weeks ago	operate	great job	accident	help	save life
now better	Best wishes				

Dear Superheroes,

1 Read and answer the questions.

It is always important to tell the truth. But there are some times in life when it's not the best thing to do. These times are usually when we don't want to hurt other people's feelings. The truth can sometimes make other people feel bad or unhappy. Not telling the truth is called 'telling a lie'. When we do this because we don't want to hurt someone, it's called 'telling a little white lie' and it's OK.

1 How can telling the truth sometimes make people feel? _____

2 Why do we tell little white lies? _____

3 Do you ever tell little white lies? _____

4 When was the last time you told a little white lie? _____

2 Imagine a situation and write about telling a little white lie.

It was ...

1 Write the sentences and questions.

1 I / help / can / my / friend? / How   How can I help my friend?
2 tell / didn't / I / the / truth
3 speak / should / Who / he / to?
4 friend / best / in / cheats / My / exams
5 really / big / made / I've / mistake / a
6 do? / should / I / What

2 Read the letter and answer the questions.

Dear Betty and Robert,

I'm worried about my friend, Peter. He's got some new friends at school and they like doing bad things. Peter really wants to be part of their group. They told him to go to the shopping centre and steal some things. Peter doesn't feel that this is wrong. He has started to take little things from a small shop near home. He says he's practising because there are a lot of cameras in the big shopping centre. I told him that this group of boys aren't really his friends and that the police can catch him, but he doesn't want to listen and laughs at me. He thinks it's a joke. What should I do?

Yours,

Daisy

1 How can Daisy help Peter?   She should
2 Who can Daisy talk to?
3 Should Daisy tell Peter's parents?
4 Should Daisy tell a teacher?

3 Write a reply to Daisy.

85

Grammar reference

1 Write the times.

1 `7.20` Jim got up at <u>twenty past seven</u> .

2 `7.45` He had a shower at _____ .

3 `7.55` He got dressed at _____ .

4 `8.05` He ate his breakfast at _____ .

5 `8.25` He went to school at _____ .

6 `8.50` He arrived at school at _____ .

2 Read and write.

1 They're going to play tennis. (hockey) <u>No, they aren't. They're going to play hockey.</u>

2 She's going to eat some cheese. (meat) _____

3 He's going to have lunch at school. (home) _____

4 We're going to get up early. (late) _____

5 I'm going to buy a new CD. (comic) _____

6 It's going to rain. (snow) _____

3 Read and choose the right words.

1 She rode her bike (**along**) / **left** the road.
2 They drove **past** / **right** the school.
3 He took the fourth street on the **straight on** / **right**.
4 The museum was **across** / **corner** the street.
5 I turned **straight on** / **left** at the post office.
6 The bus stopped at the **corner** / **across**.

4 Read and order the words.

1 [his] [George wasn't] [homework.] [doing]

<u>George wasn't doing his homework.</u>

2 [in the] [Sarah skiing] [mountains?] [Was]

_____

3 [I] [bath.] [having a] [wasn't]

_____

4 (to an) (sailing) (island.) (David was)

   ----

5 (Emma and Harry) (the park.) (through) (were running)

   ----

6 (the bus stop?) (Were) (waiting at) (you)

   ----

5 Answer the questions.

1 What are these bowls made of? (relvis)   _They're made of silver._____
2 What's this comic made of? (reppa)   _____
3 What are his shoes made of? (threale)   _____
4 What's her scarf made of? (lowo)   _____
5 What are windows made of? (sagls)   _____
6 What's that watch made of? (logd)   _____

6 Complete the sentences.   (like   cheese   It   feel   ~~tired~~)

1 She looked _tired_____ .   4 We didn't _____ sad.
2 They tasted _____ mangoes.   5 _____ doesn't sound very nice.
3 It smelled like _____ .

7 Read and write 'Yes, you should.' or 'No, you shouldn't.'

1 Should you leave your rubbish on the ground?   _No, you shouldn't._____
2 Should you play your music very loudly?   _____
3 Should you use sun cream when you go to the beach?   _____
4 Should you play with animals in fields?   _____
5 Should you wear strong shoes when you walk in the mountains?   _____
6 Should you drink water from a river?   _____

8 Write questions and answers.

1 she / ever / climb / mountain? (✓) _Has she ever climbed a mountain?_ _Yes, she has._
2 they / ever / enter / competition? (✗) _____ _____
3 he / ever / play / table tennis? (✗) _____ _____
4 they / ever / make / snowman? (✓) _____ _____
5 you / ever / see / the Olympics? (✗) _____ _____

87

Irregular verbs

Infinitive	Past tense	Past participle
be	was / were	been
be called	was / were called	been called
be going to	was / were going to	been going to
begin	began	begun
break	broke	broken
bring	brought	brought
buy	bought	bought
can	could	–
catch	caught	caught
choose	chose	chosen
come	came	come
cut	cut	cut
do	did	done
draw	drew	drawn
drink	drank	drunk
drive	drove	driven
dry	dried	dried
eat	ate	eaten
fall	fell	fallen
fall over	fell over	fallen over
feel	felt	felt
find	found	found
find out	found out	found out
fly	flew	flown
forget	forgot	forgotten
get	got	got
get (un)dressed	got (un)dressed	got (un)dressed
get (up / on / off)	got (up / on / off)	got (up / on / off)
get to	got to	got to
give	gave	given
go	went	gone / been
go out	went out	gone / been out
go shopping	went shopping	gone / been shopping
grow	grew	grown
have	had	had
have got	had	had
have (got) to	had to	had to
hear	heard	heard
hide	hid	hidden
hit	hit	hit
hold	held	held
hurt	hurt	hurt
keep	kept	kept
know	knew	known

Infinitive	Past tense	Past participle
learn	learnt / learned	learnt / learned
leave	left	left
let	let	let
lie down	lay down	lain down
lose	lost	lost
make	made	made
make sure	made sure	made sure
mean	meant	meant
meet	met	met
must	had to	had to
put	put	put
put on	put on	put on
read	read	read
ride	rode	ridden
run	ran	run
say	said	said
see	saw	seen
sell	sold	sold
send	sent	sent
should		
sing	sang	sung
sit	sat	sat
sleep	slept	slept
smell	smelt / smelled	smelt / smelled
speak	spoke	spoken
spell	spelt / spelled	spelt / spelled
spend	spent	spent
stand	stood	stood
steal	stole	stolen
swim	swam	swum
swing	swung	swung
take	took	taken
take a photo / picture	took a photo / picture	taken a photo / picture
take off	took off	taken off
teach	taught	taught
tell	told	told
think	thought	thought
throw	threw	thrown
understand	understood	understood
wake up	woke up	woken up
wear	wore	worn
win	won	won
write	wrote	written